Online or Offline Business
The Ultimate Success Formula

K. Raveendran

TABLE OF CONTENTS

About this Book

This book titled "Online or Offline Business" with sub title "The Ultimate Success Formula" is written for all those individuals who wish to start a new business, either a physical store or an online store, or has already started one and has not found success so far. However, more emphasis has been given to Online business as running a physical store does not require much explanation.

This book will be beneficial for all those who wish to start a genuine business, according to the law of the land and want to earn a decent income. The information given in this book will help you save time; money and energy so that you can concentrate on the main task, that is, start your business as early as possible with the right products, tools, and services, which in turn will increase your Return on Energy (RoE) as well as Return on Investments (RoI).

It also cover topics like marketing and promotion, social media networking, useful tips, and outsourcing difficult jobs, safety and security. You can be rest assured that they are reliable, trustworthy, and useful.

I will walk you through every aspect of starting a business right from identifying a business through research and analysis including product selection, sourcing products, market platforms/sales channels, essential tools including analytics. Thus, you will be able to learn the whole gamut of starting, nurturing and growing a business from scratch and how you can take advantage of various technologies for achieving your goal.

Chapter 1

INTRODUCTION

Most new businesses fail in the first three months of starting it, due to lack of knowledge of the business they are into, no or little experience in sales and marketing. In addition, wrong selection of products and sales channel, not putting in the required amount of time and effort, does not know who their customers are, or what is their customers profile viz, age, gender, profession, income group, geography etc.

The main reason for failure of the venture is that most individuals start a business without having a business plan, which covers the topics like what product or service they are going to provide. Investment and infrastructure requirement, nature and type of business, location, financial needs, legal procedures, etc. They also do not have any idea about conducting proper research, investigations, and surveys about the demand for their product or service.

Another reason for failure of a new businesses is starting a business without checking their aptitude in business and not identifying their Strength, Weakness, Opportunity, and Threats (SWOT analysis). They think that people will accept the goods or services they are offering, because they like it very much and thought other people will buy it from them immediately.

This is foolishness. Since you like the product very much, it is not necessary that other people will like your product and buy it from you.

Sometimes the product may have excellent features and high technology. However, an ordinary person may not understand the technicalities of the goods and hence may not be interested in knowing its great features. What the customer is interested in is, how beneficial the goods or services are to him/her and its cost i.e. the usefulness of the product or service and affordability, nothing else.

That means irrespective of the great features, BENEFITS always sells and not Features.

An Individual who wish to start his/her own business, first do some online searches get some free eBooks or buy them at unreasonable high prices. Sometimes, very cheap materials, provided by the so-called gurus, whose means are questionable and difficult to verify the accuracy of their claims and authenticity. However, there may be a few exceptions, majority of the cases are frauds.

In your quest for getting the best information and best products, you keep on searching the internet, buy more and more e-books or training videos, podcasts, DVDs etc, and end up as a pauper. What happens? Over a period, your quest for perfection, makes you restless, frustrated and because of information overload, you lose faith in the system and curse your fate. You will not take any action and end up in failure.

Imagine the amount of time, money, and efforts wasted in perfecting your knowledge for the elusive best business model that can give you the highest return on investment (RoI), in the shortest possible time. I want to help you save your valuable time, money and most importantly do things with lesser efforts.

Have you ever thought about what type of material you are getting? How useful are they in your daily life, profession, or business? Most types of materials either are out dated or crap. It will not help you or lead anywhere. The type of e-books and videos available on the internet are related to multi level marketing (MLM), Pay per Click, Affiliate Marketing, Google Ads, Cost Per Action (CPA), Paid Surveys, Typing job, Cost Per View (CPV), Creating and Selling e-Books and Videos related to innumerable goods and services.

There is no dearth of such schemes floating on the internet. Women are the most victims of this type of frauds, because they are mostly work at home moms. Don't have much exposure or experience in a particular field. Want to earn their livelihood from the proposed business and/or supplement their meager income. The above types of business are mostly scams, and may not help you earn any money, except it helps the person who started it. Therefore, my humble request to the prospective entrepreneurs are not to give attention to this type of schemes and waste your precious time and money.

Warning

Just because I have provided all the necessary inputs for starting a successful business, please do not take it for granted that by merely following the information contained in this book will ensure your success, because success of a business depends on many factors. Therefore, my dear friends do not forget to do your home work well. There is no guarantee that your venture will succeed instantly. Success depends on factors like, your dedication, investment capacity, right selection of goods and services, economic (market) conditions, government policies , laws and regulations.

In addition, demand and supply, obsolete technology, your experience in the field, and various other factors, and to some extent, your luck. My intention here is to warn you beforehand so that you will not be in the illusion that

3

just because someone told that you start this business and you can earn millions instantly.

There is no magic, no short cut, but dedication, perseverance and sticking to basic principles of business, you can definitely succeed in your venture and reach the pinnacle.

Above all, experience, especially in sales and marketing, matters a lot in the success of your business, both brick and mortar or online. However, not be discouraged by my warning.

Even if you have no experience, but can put in the required efforts to learn on your own or if you can afford to employ, capable person(s) to run the business, then also you can succeed, but do not forget your overall supervision is essential.

Chapter 2

THE BASICS

Even before you start searching for a business idea or product, it is better to do an entrepreneurial aptitude test ETA or Self-assessment test to assess your entrepreneurial ability score and know where you stand. Whether you have the aptitude/ability to be an entrepreneur and if not what you need to learn.

You can get it done online through a web search and take a free test. "Just type free online entrepreneurial aptitude test", lo you are presented with several sites that provide free ETA test, chose one of the listed sites and take the test. This will ensure that you will not waste any time and money in case you do not have any business aptitude.

The thought of starting a business of your own is very exciting and have been there in your mind for some time and it might not have popped out suddenly. Whatever are the reasons and the circumstances, a person who decides to be an entrepreneur, have certain innate qualities inherent in him or her. What are those qualities or traits? The foremost of them is the desire to be his or her own master, no boss, no reporting, no time limit, and no deadline. Above all, have the capacity to take reasonable risks involved in running a business.

However, all these people have one thing in common i.e. the burning desire to succeed in life through hard work, dedication and lead a dignified and qualitative life, but own their own terms. Thinking of starting your own business is OK, but there are certain specific qualities required to be successful in a business of your own. You must be ready to put in the required amount of work either through own efforts or getting it done through someone else.

Irrespective of the means used, you need to dedicate yourself for the success of your venture. Be it be trading, manufacturing, or providing a service, you cannot be lazy and need to have the perseverance and diehard spirit to succeed. Never ever, quit midway through, because winners never quit. There are many daydreamers, who think about starting a business on their own, but never take any positive action and perish.

The most successful individuals in a business are those people who have direct and long-term experience in the chosen profession, have expertise, and good in sales and marketing. They know the business inside out. Another type of people who are successful, again are those who have gained long time supervised experience in a family business set up. Their parents, siblings or expert supervisor or manager, who mended them from a younger age till such time they become familiar with the business process and are able to conduct the business on their own, with little or no support.

However, there are many third generation entrepreneurs, who successfully launched a business, say a Start up, from scratch and built an empire over a period. You do not necessarily be rich to start a business, but have the inclination and will power to succeed; especially perseverance is of utmost importance.

People like Warren Buffet, Bill Gates, or the Indian Dhirubhai Ambani etc, were all ordinary people, but grown into the top most list of rich people in the world. So don't be disheartened, you can also be successful provided you take the right decisions at the right time.

Successive surveys conducted by various agencies on the success of small or home based businesses in the United States has shown that people who venture in to own business are mostly middle aged, experienced and matured individuals in their late forties or fifties and built business from scratch and are earning an average$ 50000 to $ 100000 yearly.

Business Opportunity

An average person who jump into the band wagon of business owners are those who got some information from internet searches, or heard about some fads, or have some vague idea of the product or service they like to offer, but not having any actual experience of doing it, or do not have any sales and marketing experience.

The Startup Bandwagon

I hope you are all familiar with the term STARTUP, which is not a fancy word but describes about a new business in a single word. There are innumerable success stories of Startups that has become some of the most valuable companies in the world.

For example WhatsApp, Wework, Dropbox, Pinterest, SpaceX. DidiKuaidi, Snapchat, Plantir, Airbnb, Xiaomi, and Uber. In India, BigBazar, Ola, Flipkart, PayTm, Mobikwik etc are examples of new business become so popular and successful.

I have given the above names only to give an idea, how successful a business can be, *provided your idea of a new business is unique.* Most startups are promoted by people who have a vision and have good experience in running such entities or have learnt about the opportunity while doing other jobs.

The First Step

The first and foremost requirement for any person to be successful in a business is that he/she has good knowledge of the product or expertise in the service they plan to offer. You must have the capacity to invest the required amount of money in the business.

If someone told you that you do not need to invest anything in your own business, only your time and effort is enough, my dear friend, then it is not your business and you become a "Hawker" and not an owner of any business.

The advent of internet has changed the face of business all over the world. Irrespective of the size, whether micro, small, medium, or large scale, everybody has space out there. Normally, when it comes to business, first the picture of brick and mortar store i.e. a local shop comes in to mind. Next comes the location, traffic to the store and then all other aspects of it.

Internet based online business also fit into the same nomenclature, except the fact that it did not have a structure or a building out there, instead you see WebPages, with a domain name, that is your business identity and all other details like name of business, contact details, product or service details, terms and conditions, privacy policy, etc.

The Basics

Since you have some idea about the type of business you like to start, based on your experience and knowledge, it would be a good idea to do some basic research to find out whether there is any actual demand for the product or service that you wish to offer. If so, whether there is enough demand and profitability in order to sustain your business.

Types of Business

There are three types of businesses, you can choose from, viz. Proprietorship firm, partnership firm, and body incorporate, depending upon your investment capacity, and over all experience.

Proprietorship Firm

As the name indicates, proprietorship firms are solely owned by an individual and he or she has total control of the business. This type of business suits small ventures requiring low investments. E.g. are retail shops, food vending outlets, bakery, photo studio, online retail stores, small trading firms and so on. While registering with the tax authorities, it requires only fewer forms.

Partnership Firm

Partnership firms typically consist of two or more partners and mostly in the family business. Some examples are legal, taxation, and trading firms. There are different types of partnerships viz. general partnership, limited liability partnerships. Normally, an agreement is made and registered, indicting the amount each partner invested, his/her share of ownership, who conducts the business and sharing of responsibility, sharing profits, all these are mentioned clearly in the agreement. In case of death of any one of the partners, or insolvency, the firm becomes invalid.

Corporation

Corporation type of business is body incorporate or popularly known as corporate entities with shareholding by individuals, firms and the public. The firm may be a public limited or a private limited company. They have to register with the registrar of companies or similar entities in different countries. They can issue shares, and transfer ownership easily. This type of business requires large investments and consists of three or more directors.

Business Categories

There are three categories of businesses viz. information products, physical products and services. Based on your profile, interests, and experience level, select the one that suits you the most. If you know beforehand, where you are going, then you will be able to reach your destination easily. Similarly, if you know what type of business suits you, then you will be able to plan accordingly.

Information Products

Info (rmation) products are most suited for people who have specialized and have in-depth knowledge in a particular field: e.g. arts and crafts, fitness, music, dance, sales and marketing, astrology, gemology, novelist, cookery, and soon. The list is endless and your imagination is the limit. There are innumerable opportunities in different fields, which you can utilize to monetize your talent by producing different types of information (digital) products e.g. a training video, a podcast, a pdf file or an e-book, a CD or DVD and so on.

Physical Products

Physical products are goods used in our daily life like, books both academic and referral, fiction, non-fiction, comic; electronic and electrical goods, TV, camera, jewellery, beauty and cosmetics, apparel, household goods like kitchen and tableware, food, interior, furniture, furnishing, garden, automobile parts, and such other products running into several thousands of categories.

Services

Examples of services are: A web designer, a content writer, an SEO specialist, a graphic designer, a tutor, an attorney, a tax advisor, a dentist, a composer, an insurance advisor, an app developer, a real estate agent, and so on. You can offer your services locally, nationally or internationally, either offline in a physical location or through the media of internet to interested parties for a fee, on hourly work basis or project as a whole basis.

How to Identify a Business Opportunity

To identify a business opportunity is to look around you, e.g. shopping places, magazines, newspaper ads and reports, articles, blogs or online shopping sites. However, the best place is the internet, where you can do search and find out search volumes, geography, demography, customer profiles like, gender, age, education, income, where they shop, etc.

You can also find out the products or service that has got demand and if so, is there any profitability for that particular product. Note down your findings in to a notebook or diary to record your research details.

The next step is to go to major search engines viz. Google, Yahoo, Bing, AOL, or shopping engines, popularly known as comparison sites, and do a search using your keywords or phrases.

For example, talking melody radio, or Cannon SLR digital camera, when you search for the result, look in the search box, there appears many words and phrases, note them all into your book or diary. Normally you get about 4 to 6 words and phrases for each keyword you type in the search box and an auto search result page will be appearing in front of you i.e. the page on which you find different web site names.

In Google, the search result shows ten (10) results at a time,[excluding the sponsored advertisements, on the top, normally three, bottom and right side panel with the same keywords or keyword phrases].In addition, you can see several search related queries appearing on the bottom of the page.

In Yahoo search, you can see more results. You can do further research by clicking on the site names appearing there and refine your search. Do it one at a time. In case you are not satisfied with the resultant page, go to the next page and so on and if you are not satisfied, use another key word or phrase i.e. any variation or combination of words and phrases.

Note down all the keywords and phrases that you like and take only the top ones related to your product or service. The next step is to find out the best articles based on the key words related to your product or service and find out what product or service they are promoting there. The best places are Article Directories, Web 2 properties, blogging platforms, Video, Photo, and Slide share sites.

Do not forget to note down all the keywords or phrases used there in the article and videos, its headings, and sub-headings. You can also get ideas from Yahoo trends, Google trends, Bing (MSN) trends, etc. where on the home pages of the above search engines you can see lots of information that you can use for your new business. In addition, you can also get business or product ideas from shopping sites/comparison sites popularly known as shopping engines.

Once you have about 25-30 keywords or phrases, then, go to Google Planner, the keyword research tool (which is free) and then use Google Trends to find out the geography and trends of the searches and search percentages. In the search results, you can see the number of monthly and global searches, SEO competition, cost per click, click through rate, and so on.

It will be a good idea to do further research about the customer profile like age, gender, education, income, location, price at which they will be interested in your product or services. There are no better places than Alexa.com, Compete.com, and Quantcast.com to get the details. Though they all give detailed information free of cost, however, some of the extra information may be available only on payment or subscription basis. You can find out those details from their web site.

Chapter 3

THE BUSINESS PLAN

The next big step is to prepare your business plan. This should include every aspect of your proposed business e.g. nature and type of business - whether it is a proprietorship, partnership, or body incorporate. A trading, manufacturing, or providing a service or you wants to start a store at a physical location, or an online store or both.

The Business Plan should include details such as the product you plan to sell, income and expenditure statement, profitability statement, geography of operation like, local, national or international, mode of operation etc.

In addition, you may need to have sales, marketing and promotional plans, source of funds, recurring and fixed expenses like cost of the goods i.e. stocks, fixed assets like computer, software and other tools and services, in certain cases, machinery, rent, electricity and so on.

Even if you are starting a brick and mortar store i.e. a physical shop, in this era of electronic transactions, you will need credit/debit card transaction facility. Otherwise, you will be losing huge amount of business from this segment. In order to facilitate card payment you will have to use payment gateways from banks or other providers including Mobile swipe facility. There will be deposits for the swipe machine or mobile swipe machine in addition to transaction fees.

The average cost per transaction is around 2% for credit cards and around 1.80% for debit cards. This can vary slightly up or down, you have to find out the best fees from different providers and get the best one that suits your budget, but do not compromise on quality of service.

In case of online stores, expenses towards listing fee, transaction fee, store front, web hosting, domain name, payment gateway and shopping cart, web site maintenance (CMS), salaries for staff or for self to meet expenses, taxes to be paid etc.). Also, sales and marketing expenses, office expenses like telephone, broadband internet subscription, email, postage, transportation, maintenance and other miscellaneous expenses.

In addition, you have to make provisions for insurance–both medical and life, for your family as well as for shop, in case it is a physical store, or manufacturing unit. In case of manufacturing units, you have to get a comprehensive insurance, covering your machinery/equipments, building, raw materials, finished goods, and vehicles, if any. In addition to your business expenses, provision for regular family expenses like food, clothing, children's education, recreation, transport, electricity, gas, water and other utility bills to be provided for.

This estimate or plan should be for running the business at least for a year i.e. 12 months. In effect, you need to have funds for meeting the operational expenses as well as for meeting your family's daily needs. In case you are planning for a physical store, you need to identify the premises in a prominent place where customers can reach you easily, good flow of traffic, means customers, demand for your type of product or business in that area.

It may not be necessary to go in for all the items at once, as most small business start from the corner of your residence or garage. However, you need to have all the bare minimum tools and services for starting your business. You cannot compromise on that aspect. Your business plan must be realistic and should include expected revenue and expenditure for the next three years and ideally for the next five years. You can take the help of a chartered accountant, or alternately get the plan prepared using online facilities.

In many countries including India, there are startup hubs, both private and government owned, to encourage new businesses and you will get most of the facilities for a monthly rent, which is very reasonable and subsidized.

In case funds are limited and you are starting a very small venture, then take the help of online business plan samples and prepare the plan. This will ensure and give you an idea of how much it costs to run the business, and ensure that you don't get a shock at a later date.

Finances to meet Immediate and Recurring Expenses

How you are going to meet the expenses? From own savings or funds sourced from within your   circle of friends, relatives or from own family members like dad, mom, or siblings? If the fund requirements are high, you may like to take a loan from financial institutions like banks. For which you need to prepare a detailed business plan covering all the above areas and you may have to provide personal guarantee or collateral security for the loan amount, normally one and a half times more than the loan amount.

In the Essential Tools and Services chapter, I have given the names of some very good sources, where you can see many sample business plans and, if required, get actual business plan prepared using their services, within an hour. Don't borrow money on high interest rates; instead find out ways and means to curtail your expenses or alternatively, get funds from your own source almost free - from family members or friends. .

However, now a days, there is new a trend called **crowd funding.** If your business requires more funds, and you do not want to go to a financial institution or bank, you can get funding from like minded parties online through crowd funding sites. I am giving below a few names of reputed and popular crowd funding sites.

1. Kickstarter
2. GoFundMe
3. Indiegogo
4. Patreon
5. Rockethub
6. GogetFunding
7. Ulule
8. CircleUp
9. Ketto (is an Indian crowd funding site)

However, please do your research and get involved with them. I have given the names in the order of their reputation. I have not tried it, but know about them.

Note

This should be your motto "Start small, settle down, and grow". When you earn enough profits, established in the market, and have steady business and good flow of funds, then you can get a loan from banks at reasonable interest rates.

Once the above details are finalized, the next step is to decide about your business, whether it is retail, wholesale, or a combination of both. The structure of the business brick and mortar or an internet based online store or both. If it is a brick and mortar store, you need to give prominence to the selection of location and success rate of the particular type of business in that location.

Sometimes, the location is excellent, but your type of product or service has never succeeded in that location. Therefore, identify a location that is easy to access, have good flow of customers (traffic) to the shop, and are successful in that location. Please get a survey done by you or got it done through college or business management students. However, the best way to get a survey done is by using the service of a professional agency. This will cost you a little more but worth it. For online stores, you must use reputed survey companies like survey monkey etc.

In case of online or internet store, use an excellent sales platform/market places like eBay, Amazon or other third party shopping carts. The storefront must have good, hosting, 99.9% uptime, a good look and feel, a Shopping cart and Payment gateway, good customer service facility like live chat, a contact telephone number, interactive suggestion tools, Security features like SSL certificate, preferably with Extended Validation(the domain name with secure lock and https://www.yourname.com highlighted in green light), and fraud protection.

If affordable, use the verified by Visa, Master Card, or Amex facility and also use the privacy protection logos like VeriSign, McAfee and the trust logs like BBB, TRUSTe. However, most reputed payment gateways offer the verified by Visa, Master Card, Amex, Outlook etc. in their shopping cart package.

The next step is to start writing content for your web pages with right amount of key word spread, graphics, sitemap, internal links, and proper navigation. Need not worry, if you are not familiar with all these aspects, you can get things done using the free web site builder (if you are able to do it yourself), otherwise by outsourcing everything at reasonable cost.

While designing your web site, attention should be given to minute details like, the purpose of your web site, structure, navigational aspects, internal and external links, color schemes browsing compatibility, both desktop, notebook and mobile browsing. Mobile and Tablet usage has overtaken the conventional browsing since mobile is the current buzzword. It would be a better idea to have a single web page design compatible with both conventional desktop/ notebook and mobile users alike; otherwise, it can cause difficulty to your users. Keeping this in mind, use Responsive Templates designed incorporating HTML5, CSS3, and SEO features.

Important Tips

Outsource everything at the first time to avoid mistakes and smooth running of your web store. Thereafter, you can learn the tricks slowly and do it yourself, if you have the time. Otherwise, engage someone experienced or outsource the CMS (content management service) to people who can do it, at reasonable cost.

Alternatively, use readymade all-in-one solutions; you get everything needed to run your online business - domain name, web hosting, web page design (DIY),do it yourself i.e. no technical jargons like HTML, CSS, SEO, shopping cart, payment gateway, analytics, social marketing, PPC management and so on.

Don't use any hosting company's domain, especially, a free one along with the package, because most of the time the domain name may not be in your name, but in their name. Second reason is that it will be easy for you to shift the domain to any other host, if need arises.

Chapter 4

MARKET PLATFORM

Once you have decided about the type of business you like to start, viz. Information products, Physical products, or Services. Select the appropriate sales channel i.e. Market Platform, like popular shopping sites or your own independent web store.

In case you are selling services, you can buy a domain name and a hosting account (buy both from different providers) from reputed domain and hosting providers. You also need a payment gateway for collecting payment. You can choose the one you like the most from a host of providers.

It is better to choose a hosting provider from your own country, if possible, as it will be easy to deal with them in case something goes wrong later. The following are some of the best places, where you can start your online businesswise. Amazon, eBay and other reputed shopping sites. A list of top rated shopping and shopping comparison sites are given in the chapter dealing with Essential Tools and Services. You may select anyone of them that you feel suits you the most.

Do not forget to choose a shopping cart provider (especially with a built in blog feature included in the package). This is very important, since you can use the blog(a business blog and not a personal blog) for various purposes, like conducting an audience poll, a survey, brand building, product promotion, and traffic generation.

Information Products

If you are an infoprenuer selling information (digital) products like an eBook, a DVD, a CD, an Audio, or a Music album, there are large numbers of platforms, through which you can sell your creations. There is no other form of businesses that requires virtually no investment or little investment except your time, for creating and perfecting the product and sell the finished product in digital form through a variety of channels, viz. exclusive online or offline digital product selling shops and physical bookstores.

However, there are certain important aspects you need to know and adhere to before submitting your product for selling. The most important factor is that you should format your eBook in the required format so that it can be accessed in any form of browsers, like desktop, mobile or tablets.

The most popular formats are: .epub, .pdf, .ibook (Apple), Kindle (Amazon), .mobi (Mobile pocket) , and Mp3/4 (audio products). Pictures or graphics need to be provided in .jpg, or.jpeg format, and videos must be in the .wmv, .avi, .mov, and.mpg/.mpeg3, and .flv (.flv is for flash video player). As regards graphics are concerned, the popular formats are .jpg or .jpeg, .tiff, and .gif. My dear friends, seeing all these things, do not get frightened. In case you are not familiar with all this, you can get necessary help from your eBook distributors.

Most of the reputed online eBook and digital product distributors and large retailers have their own tools to help you convert your document into the required file format to enable your eBook and other products in different browser interfaces. You can sell your products directly through your own web site or through a blog

21

site, even through your social networking sites, in addition to selling your product through a large network of online distributors and retailers, both small and large.

Some of the most popular places you can sell your products are Kindle (Amazon), Smashwords, Kobo, iBookstore (Apple), and Barnes and Noble. These are some of the top rated and most reputed eBook sales and distribution places, where you can sell your information/digital products. A complete list of most popular and reputed digital product distribution channel names are given in the chapter dealing with Essential Tools and Services. You can browse through the same and choose the ones you like the most. You can also sell on auction sites like eBay as an auctioneer or a fixed price seller.

Amazon is also a very good place to sell info products. They have various platforms, fully loaded with features, which are hassle free and simple to use. Above all, includes all the tools you require to run an online business including payment collection and delivery.

My dear fellow writers and other digital product creators please do not expect miracles immediately after submitting your eBook, music album, or podcast material to online distributors for selling. It takes time for customers to find your product. At times, it can happen that you may not even sell a single piece of your product. Blame it on your luck, fate or otherwise. However, the real fact is that new writers need to create awareness about yourself and your product amongst buyers.

How do you do that?

The answer is simple! You have to market yourself much before your product reaches the market. Many new writers and musicians and other specialists like photographers, short film producers make the mistake of not marketing themselves. The result is that no one knows you.

How to Promote You and Your Products

In order to create brand awareness about you and your products, you need to start promoting yourself. Again, many people think that it is a big problem! How can I afford so much of money to spend on advertising? My dear fellow infopreneurs please do not panic, just because I mentioned that you must promote yourself, I did not ask you to spend any money on advertising. My intention is that you start promoting yourself using most available free channels like social media networks, business blogs and Web2 properties text messaging, and press releases using free press release agencies.

Social media networks alone can give you about 25-40% business and they are places where you can find your customers through networking and interaction. Once you have earned some money you can go for paid promotions. Until then, be within your limits.

If you borrow money from someone, it can create difficult situations in future, because liabilities are frightening. Details about promoting you and your business are given in the Essential Tools, and Services chapter.

Tip No.1

Never ever go for a paid service for listing your digital products for distribution to retail selling channels. There are several online distributors charging a fee for membership to their sites. These people are not interested in promoting your products, but only interested in grabbing your money.

Physical Products

If you are starting a shop selling physical products, i.e. consumer goods, office supplies or industrial products, it is better to have a brick and mortar shop locally clubbed with an internet based online store. This is a must, as majority of shoppers now-a-days do product searches online or through mobile devises like Smart phones and Tablets, compare prices, benefit and features and then go and buy the product from a local store near to her.

The reason behind this attitude is, a buyer want to see the product physically and then feel about the product and buy it. Above all, she feels more comfortable to buy locally, because, in case she needs a service, she can get it very fast locally. Even if a refund problem arises, it is easy to deal with a local vendor.

For selling physical products online, there is no other place than Amazon. They are awesome, the pioneers and market leader of the highest quality and service. This is my first choice for starting an online trading platform for selling physical products. Even if you have a brick and mortar shop, you can sell the same or different products online using Amazon's facilities either by listing your products there or as separate store.

Here is an example. A friend of mine who runs a wholesale photographic goods store in my city started selling the film rolls using Amazon facility initially and later on to the complete range of products including cameras. I have seen personally, they engaged two girls to pack and send the films to Amazon storage point. When checked with the owner, he told me that on an average his daily film roll sales is around 50 pieces whereas he was selling a few pieces prior to joining online trade. Therefore, please do not ignore the power of online sales as it gives the opportunity to sell across the country.

Amazon

Why Amazon? There are innumerable shopping sites out there. Why should you go with Amazon? You asked a good question! Primarily, Amazon is the pioneer in online product selling and the Number One integrated online shopping site. They are the oldest, largest, and most trustworthy business group online. Amazon operates in the USA and Canada, UK, France, Germany, Italy, Spain, Japan, India and China. Through Amazon you can sell in any particular country, region or globally.

They have a large satisfied customer base. Offers everything you need to start a new business, including basic training, product packing, labeling and delivery all that, of course, for a fee. There is no free lunch. Remember that nothing comes free in this world. Selling on Amazon is child's play. It is very easy. They have tailor made programs: Web Store by Amazon, Amazon Web Services (AWS), Fulfillment by Amazon (FBA) and Amazon Prime. All the services are based on a listing fee and sales commission and fees for using FBA. The various fee charged by Amazon can be found from their site at Sellers Central. Here is a brief description of various Amazon programs.

Fulfillment by Amazon (FBA)

FBA is an integrated service offered by Amazon. They will pick, pack, store and ship inventory, handle returns, provide excellent customer service, and collect payments on your behalf. Currently FBA services are available in the United States, Germany, United Kingdom, Italy, China, France, and India.

Amazon FBA offers many benefits to sellers like, free super saving shipping in the US, EU and Japan, and Amazon Prime and other expedited shipping options, that will reduce your shipping costs and delivery time substantially.

FBA offers another excellent service i.e. Multi-channel fulfillment. That means, in addition to Amazon, you can use FBA services for other channels like eBay, or your own web store.

Another excellent service from Amazon is the FBA Export. Using this service you can export eligible products to supported countries in the US and EU. These include DVD, Music, Books, and Videos using fulfillment by multi-channel FBA. For example, in the EU region, you can export from one member country to another from a single fulfillment centre without moving the goods from one country to another, where Amazon currently operates with a unified seller account i.e. using the European Fulfillment service network.
Amazon Prime

Amazon Prime is a membership program, currently with an annual membership fee. They are eligible for free delivery based on certain minimum purchase and you get delivery within 2 days.

Amazon Web Store

Web Store by Amazon is a separate platform for selling physical products, i.e. like your own independent web store, but hosted on Amazon Web Services (AWS) platform.

Product Selection

Amazon is an enormous giant, selling various items on its own. Then how will you find product to sell in competition with it? There is huge demand for various products; people are ready to buy from Amazon. My advice to prospective new entrepreneurs is not to promote any high value products in competition with Amazon and its competitors, especially in the initial stages. Instead, select a micro-niche of any product group, and sell as a specialist.

Start by selling low priced, in demand products, and once you gain sufficient knowledge and expertise, then go and sell most popular and high value products.

Tip No.2

When selling high value products like cameras, TVs, smart phones, tablets etc. and most popular categories like electronics, please remember that a newbie cannot compete with the giants unless you have the resources and expertise. However, you can add value to the main product with accessories or related combination product offers. This way, you can earn a decent profit out of a sale.

How do you know which product sell and which product not? Here you need to find out from Amazon categories, which are the hot favorites, which items sell fast, what type of deals are offered there, their pricing, etc. How other sellers compete with Amazon and sell their own products through Amazon.

With the training you get from Amazon Sellers Central and the Sellers Forum, you will be able to get all these details. In addition, you can use analytical tools to find out important market information like, pricing, demography, title used, product range etc. and sell in competition with fellow high flyers.
Important Tip

Selling on Amazon is mostly influenced by the Seller Ratings i.e. the number of Stars, 1 to 5, comments and feed backs you get. Therefore, as soon as you finish a sale, contact your customer and ask for feedbacks, comments or a rating on the site.

India Specific Information

In 2016 Government of India started a scheme for helping Startups in India with a found size of Rupees 10000 crores, as incubation hub and startup training centers spread across different cities.

The scheme at present consists of 50 categories which includes, Electronics and information technology, bio-technology, software development, IPR and others mostly comes under the MSME category under the overall control of different ministries and departments. You can get complete information here at www.startupindiahub.org.in.

In India there are several big and small online Market Platforms. However, the big two players are Amazon and Flipkart. Both of them are well established and compete with each other. However, through innovative movements Amazon has established as the Number One e-Retailing Platform in India. Amazon did not require any introduction here. Flipkart started operations early in India and after several acquisitions and mergers it has been leading in Indian market. However, after the entry of Amazon into full time operation, it challenged the superiority of Flipkart and outnumbered it to become the number one online retailing platform in India.

eBay

eBay is the largest online auction site. You can sell any type of products, viz. used, new etc. They charge a listing fee and volume sales commission; you can also list products category, for a monthly fee. eBay operates in 22 countries spread across the Asia Pacific, Europe, and North America. Therefore, you must have a portfolio of products selling in eBay across the globe.

Own Web Store

The main advantage of having own website or web store is that you will have full control of your business and you don't have to share customer data, profits, commission or listing fee. Moreover, all the profits, minus expenses are yours. However, if you are not well experienced in selling online, then this may not be a good idea at the beginning.

Otherwise, you can go alone and do everything on your own including, choosing your domain, hosting, site design, sales and marketing, social media management, content management, collection of payments, and all other related functions. However, I will not suggest you to stop selling on Amazon and eBay, for the simple reason that it offers enormous business opportunity and profit potential.

Services

For selling service as a business, you don't need anything else other than, a web site with your own domain name, a good web hosting and a payment processing service. A domain name costs about $ 10 a year and a good web hosting between $5 and $10 a month. The payment processing fee varies from provider to provider, which is between 2.0 percent to 5.0 percent for each transaction or sale value for digital products and physical products.

If you are selling subscriptions, the fee varies from 7.0 percent to 15.0 percent. In addition, you need to know how to market your services to prospective customers. More details are available in the chapter dealing with Marketing and Promotion.

Special Note for Service Sellers

If you are a service seller, i.e. specialized service providers like a graphic designer, a logo designer, a web designer, or a Photoshop/Adobe illustrator and so on, then in addition to your own web site or place selling your service you can sell your services through crowd sourcing sites.

As the name indicates, crowd sourcing is a place where many service providers compete with each other and offer designs or service to a buyer and the buyer choose the best one as per his/her choice and pay for the same. The site owner will take a cut for his service i.e. about10 to 20 percent from the fee he/she collects from the customer and the rest goes to the designer/service provider.

Some best crowd sourcing sites are:

Mycrowdburst.com
Crowdspring.com
Designcrowd.com
Odesk.com
Freelancelance.com (one of the largest, but be careful they have a subscription scheme, which I do not think one must enter into. However, if you feel, and worth it, then it is OK, otherwise not).

Chapter 5

PRODUCT SOCURCING

You can start from your local wholesaler or small- scale manufacturer and then extend it to your State or Country level suppliers before venturing into international arena. That you can do when you have gained sufficient experience and know, how to procure from international suppliers both shipping and wholesale suppliers.

India Specific Information

Doing business in India has changed a lot with the arrival of a new government led by Narendra Modi in 2014. The government made it more easier doing business in India and simplified registration and license procedures. With the introduction of new GST in 2017, across India there is only one tax rate and this has further simplified procurement from any part of India. In January 2018, Government of India removed the restrictions on establishing 100% single brand direct retailing stores in India, by Foreign Direct Investment. .

In India the popular wholesale markets are Delhi, Munbai, Surat, Kolkotta, Tiruppur, Kochi, Jaipur. However, there are specific markets for various products. For example, if you want to procure readymade garments, Delhi, Mumbai and Bangalore are the places you can procure them.

Similarly, for woolen items, Ludhiana, sports goods, Jalandhar, Sarees and Dress materials, Surat, knitwear, Tiruppur, Silk sarees, Varanasi and Kancheepuram. Gem and Jewellery, handicrafts and handmade items, Jaipur. The list is unednding. You can procure fabrics, handloom and handicrafts from various state and Central Government corporations.

There are also various specialized markets for thousands of items. The Indiamart.com is a good place to search for different items, including manufacturers, growers, and wholesalers of different goods.

For getting information about wholesale fruits and vegetable marks and other information about agriculture produce, you can get it from the following web sites i.e.Data.gov.in and kisan.gov.in Further, if you are keen to source organic food that include grains, fruits and vegetables and legumes the most authentic web site is of that of ofai.org. From this site, you can get state wise list of farmers producing different food items.

Now that you have identified a product or service, you have all the details of your customer. Before going forward any further, please decide the type of business that you are going to start, ownership type, whether a proprietorship or partnership firm or a body incorporate.

Whatever be the type of ownership, you need to know certain important aspects of your business, like registration of your business with local/state bodies, laws pertaining to your trade, tax liability, filing of tax returns and payment of tax, banking account, sales tax and VAT/GST registration, export or import license requirements, excise laws and tariffs, customs duty etc.

Information about the procedure to followed, amount payable, type of license required and things like that can be found out from your local municipal office or tax authorities, in your state/country or even from their web site. Each state, country, or region has its own laws and requirements.

Therefore, it is better to get all these information before starting your business i.e. if you know all the rules and regulations, procedures and liabilities, it saves you time, money and effort in addition any surprises in future. This not only gives you an advantage, but also can help you succeed in your business, because knowledge guarantees success.

In India, as per the new procedure, you can get your registration and license through online portal of government of India.

Registration, Licenses and Bank Account

Register your firm or business name with local tax authorities and/or municipal authority, get your trade license/firm registration certificate, Sales Tax, and VAT/GST registration number.

Open a bank account preferably a current account with a pass book/statement facility, international Credit and Debit Card. If you are planning to sell on the international markets (most online stores sell internationally), you need to get an export and/or import license number [known as IEC number].

Internet related Tools and Services

A domain name, web design service, business hosting account, payment gateway, market place/ shopping cart, SSL certificate, and fraud protection.

Writing content for your web site based on the product or service that you like to promote. Research and analytical tools, product selection, demography, sales, marketing, and other related services.

It is nice to hear that you have decided to start your own business. However, like your own kid, it is essential to take care of your business well; otherwise, you may find the going tuff and can fail miserably. In order to avoid this situation, it is better , at the beginning itself, you find a few people who can help you in starting and growing your business without any problems.

Therefore, don't fail to hire the service of a good Accountant (tax specialist) and an Attorney (lawyer). The services of these two categories of people are very essential for your business's success and getting good advice and guidance, as and when you need it. However, if you are on a tight budget, do it later.

When everything is done and ready to move forward, there comes a self-doubt. How will I proceed with? Can I afford to spend so much of money? Whether my business will be successful? If these kinds of thoughts comes to your mind, my dear friend, you are not fit for any business of your own, do something else.

Don't be a pessimist, be positive. Self-belief in your ability brings in positive energy. So forget all your worries and concentrate on your mission that is to take yourbusiness in to the world of opportunity. There may be various reasons for this state of mind. As I said at the beginning of this book, please don't worry, start small, grow your business with bare minimum investment and expand when you have enough funds and growing sales. However, don't forget to have sufficient funds for running the business even at a very low level. Otherwise, you may run into problems.

Whether you are an experienced person or a novice, when starting out in your first business, as an online storeowner, it is better to start with selling a physical product on Amazon. Once you have gained experience, start selling the same or a different product or group of products on eBay and other platforms, including your own web site. By doing small business you learn the threads and once you have gained sufficient experience in online selling, you can start your own online store and expand manifold. No one can stop you from succeeding in online selling. Until such time, lie low.

How to find products

This will be a difficult task. Where you will find right products, at the right price, quality should be good, supplier must be reliable all these things are a big problem. My dear friend, don't worry. I am here to help you find the right products through reliable supplier sources. Normally, anyone who starts a business for the first time, whether a brick and mortar shop or an online store, have mostly no idea how and where to get the goods for his or her store. You make searches in your area or nearby markets or from a dealer.

The problem is that for beginners, it may be a good experience to learn about sourcing products locally, but it is time consuming and labor intensive. You may not get good products in sufficient quantity at right quality and price.

You make a very low profit, as the margins are extremely low. You may be buying products from attics and garage sales, local artisans or storage unit auctions. All these sources are limited and may not be useful for running a store or an online business successfully for a long time. Therefore, what is the alternative? There are different types of wholesalers, viz. Light Bulk Wholesale Suppliers, Liquidation

Buying, Overstock, and Closeout Buying, Wholesale suppliers and Drop Shippers.

Light Wholesale Supplier

Light wholesale suppliers sell small affordable quantities and ship them to you. You store it in your home or sales location and then sell the products in eBay and other sales channels like Amazon.

Note: Light Bulk Wholesale channels are good for eBayers.

Liquidation Overstock and Closeout Sale

Liquidation buying is a must have channel for retailers. As the name indicates, a wholesaler or manufacturer want to liquidate his stock since they don't want to hold the stock anymore or sometimes they might have produced more quantity than required or market conditions forced them to liquidate it. In most occasions, these types of selling is either a cost-to-cost sale or sometimes at a loss sale. However, care should be taken to ensure that you get quality material. This can be an integral part of your buying sources. Close out sales may not be a regular source of buying for retailers as these are seasonal or occasional sale.

Wholesalers

Wholesalers are an integral part of selling as they have the knowledge, capacity to invest in large inventories and operates on very low margins. Different businesses use different marketing channels. For example, fast moving consumer goods (fmcg) manufacturers follow the wholesaler or C and F Agents route, and then to the Distributor- local, district or regional or an area Stockiest and then it reaches the consumer. Some businesses use the wholesaler through to the consumer and in certain type of products, manufacturer sells direct to the consumer.

Who is an Authorized Wholesaler?

Most manufacturers will be busy with manufacturing goods, which itself is a big headache, so they prefer the wholesaler route as they don't want to deal with large number of retailers. There may be some exceptions. Occasionally, you may come across a small manufacturer selling product(s) direct to you. However, most small manufacturers have limitations.

They may not be reliable. When you need large quantity of a particular item, during seasonal holidays, like Christmas, Deepawali or such festivals, it may not be available or they may not have the resources to manufacture and supply them in short notice whereas, an authorized wholesaler is more stable and reliable.

Intermediaries and Scammers

There is a saying that Buyer beware. (I mean buyer be aware). This popular adage is quite apt here as well. In your quest for getting products in a moment, sometimes dirt-cheap, on the internet sphere, you may come across large number of fraudsters and scammers in the guise of product sourcing intermediaries, product sourcing MLMs, and junk product sourcing information service and so on.

How to identify Fraudsters and Scammers?

When you come across such suspicious type of offers, viz. a web site offering without a valid proof of address, like verifiable contact details, a phone number, don't ask for a valid license or Tax ID, who makes tall claims like how much money you can make using their services, sell other services than wholesale, @ mark or IP no. instead of a domain name, these are all indications of fraudulent nature. Sometimes, they may even offer a free hosted web site as well. Therefore, keep away from such schemes.

What are the Product sourcing methods?

If you really want to succeed in physical shop or online retailing, buy products from authorized wholesalers, who sell new branded products with warranty/guarantee. There are various types of sourcing methods viz. Light Bulk Wholesaler, Wholesale Drop Shippers, Liquidation buying and Overstock/ Closeout buying, are some of the important product sourcing channels.

In India, you may be familiar with the C&F, Distributor, Stokist channels and in many of the big cities there are wholesale markets dealing in most of the products. Therefore, I do not see any difficulty for you in procurement of goods for your trade.

The same may be the case in most countries. However, if you are not able to source it locally, then there is no alternative except you source it through online sources. However, be careful in dealing with them and do your due diligence before buying anything.

How to Find Products that Sell?

As already indicated in an earlier chapter, this is a gigantic task. How to pick products for your sales. Most people get horrified, as they do not have an answer to this question. My dear fellow business friends do not get scared. Instead, find means to reach your goal.

Market Research

To identify products that sells well and can give you reasonably good profits, the best method available is through Market Research. However, an ordinary person without experience or with little experience may find it as another hurdle. If your business is online, you will use the online channels for market research. However, for physical stores, the best methods are trade directories and wholesale channels. Your immediate need is to find a product that sells well and get buyers for it.

You will go to Google, Yahoo, Bing or such popular search engines or alternatively you will go to eBay or Amazon or other shopping engines to find out what type of products are selling, which are the most in demand, level of competition, source of supply, price band, advertising, etc.

However, how do you do the research? Use automated research tools that can give you real-time results, with product information including brand name, size, range, pricing details, and competitor information. In addition, information like title keywords (the best buyer keyword) used, advertisement used, demography, and above all, when and where to sell the product in competition with the big players in the market.

Tip No.3

Most retailers sell what they like most. My dear friend, this is a most dangerous trend, because if you start selling what you like the most, you may end up pauper. Ideally, you must be able to identify what the public likes and looking for. Based on the demand, you identify the product, which will be easy to sell and earn a decent profit out of it.

Special Tools for eBay and Amazon

Normally market research is done through trial and error methods or through eBay-closed lists. However, the best method is by using Market Research and Analysis Tools. This tool is very useful in getting the starting price, especially for auction listing and Amazon sales. These tools will teach you how to do research, and get information about keywords used in the title, pricing, product category, range, supplier source, competitors, advertising methods etc.

.

How to Identify Supplier Sources

In the beginning, you can start searching for products that you intent to sell from your local small-scale manufacturers, wholesalers, and slowly, search in your state then at country level to find products that have quality, reliability of supply and marketability with reasonable profits. You can get this information either through online search, through yellow pages, trade directories, or local chambers of commerce.

However, if the products that you wish to sell are not available locally, then only, look out for product suppliers internationally. The reason is that it will be easy for you to deal with any problems that crop up with regard to quality, quantity, delivery or service matters, or even a refund. You can save lots of time and avoid frustration, if you can identify a real authorized wholesaler, preferably, verified by reputed inspection agencies, viz. Interteck, Loyyds register, or certified by D and B. SGS or similar highly reputed international agencies.

While working with wholesalers, you need to be honest about your business, viz a verifiable address, a shop or online identity, tax and VAT/GST registration, registration of firm with legal authorities, a bank account, credit card, email address and phone number.

This is necessary, because most wholesalers are honest, well established and respect genuine retailers as their customer since they look for long-term relationship and more business through product mix. A manufacturing company's authorized wholesaler is the answer for your sourcing requirement.

In India, in addition to the local wholesale markets and distributor, stockists, in the past few years large international players like Wal-Mart has opened wholesale channels meant for retailers. There are currently about 20 locations in India, where they operate. Also, the Metro has large wholesale outlets in India.

They have the resources, like sales people, warehousing space, large investment capacity and local and long distance transportation facility and distribution network. Remember, in the essential tools section, I have mentioned about reputed wholesale sources. There are free as well as paid service providers.

Though the free sources provide information, but how far they are reliable? Whereas the paid membership annual or lifetime (once) type of membership is worth its weight in gold as they provide accurate information.

Therefore, become a member and subscribe to their monthly newsletters, catalogues, promotional deals to find quality products at competitive prices. They are verified, reliable and trustworthy. There are many drop shipping companies, who will work with you and drop ship, even a single piece order.

There are several such providers offering the same type of service, but they charge a monthly subscription fee, which is not at all advisable to go in for. That will kill your profits and may not be reliable. After doing your research and found a great product, which will give you business for a long time to come and earn you good profit.

The next step is to find out a reliable source of supply. This can be an authorized wholesaler, drop shipper or even a distributor. However, precautions are necessary while selecting a wholesaler or drop shipper, as there are many unscrupulous elements out there to grab your money and vanish in thin air.

Some very important aspects of dealing with wholesalers and drop shippers are: Identity and Reputation of the Supplier. When looking for suppliers, the first thing that you should do is to find out the identity of the business, i.e. contact person, address, phone number, email, fax, website details, products dealing with, how long the entity is in business, whether it is having a physical location and so on.

Most fake suppliers are online operations and use all types of questionable means to gain your respect and trust. Buyers beware! You can get the contact details from their web site; honest and reputed suppliers provide all information on their web site. Alternatively, you can get the details from WHOIS service and match the ownership of the site or business. If you get contact phone number, Skype address, etc. contact them through different id's and phone numbers, ask for references from existing customer list.

In addition, try to find out the business details from yellow pages and local listings. Next, scrutinize the company's web site.

An internet savvy per son can easily find out a fake web site. First, the web site would not have a top domain name. There may be only few pages, lot of mistakes in the contents, uses @ in the domain name or an IP number, instead of a domain name and most of their images are, copied. These are all indications of a fake web site. So be careful. Another way to find out fraudulent suppliers are through forums. Through niche specific discussion forums, you can find out who is reliable and who is not?

There you get the opportunity to interact with people dealing in the business and well experienced people who will be able to provide information about a particular supplier and their history. An easy way to find out fake or fraudulent supplier is to ask for free samples.

Most established and trustworthy wholesalers are ready to provide samples. However, some suppliers may ask for the cost of the product. That is not an issue; at least you will come to know about the nature of the business and can find out the quality of the product. You should ask for a catalogue or brochure of their products. Most fraudulent business does not bother to have a catalog or brochure. You can also ask for an inspection of samples at the wholesaler's premises. This also gives you many opportunities to assess the supplier credentials and trustworthiness.

In case of doubt, you can look the supplier listing in eBay or Amazon to find out whether they are selling their products directly there. This will ensure the reliability of the wholesaler and their product.

To assess the reliability and quality of the product supplied buy a wholesaler is to place small orders and check the quality of the product, viz materials used, quality, reliability, and consistency of the supply, delivery time, customer care, replacement/warranty and so on.

This can help you reduce or mitigate loss. Even if the supplier turns out to be fake or substandard one, your loss will be minimal. The best way to find wholesalers is through trade fairs related to your niche. There you get to interact with the businesspersons and get first hand information about the company, their product, reputation etc.

You can also ask them in detail to find out their resources, credibility and so on. Financial History A financially sound supplier is a good choice for long-term relationship. He will be able to extend credit when good relationships are established with the supplier. He may not fret for delayed payments, if any. Whereas a debt-ridden supplier may not be able to make supplies on time, and extend credit facility because he is struggling to meet both ends.

Quality and Reliability

Meet and ask some of the supplier's customers and their aquatintants, to get first hand information about the wholesale supplier. Even if you started dealing with a particular supplier, don't forget to keep a watch on the quality of the products supplied.

Sometimes it turns out that the sample shown to or given to you is much different from that supplied to you. In addition to price, qualities of products are utmost important, including delivery schedule.

Find out the mode of payment accepted by the supplier Ask for the type of payments accepted by the wholesaler or drop shipper. Viz. credit/debit card, PayPal, Google checkout, cash on delivery or a cheque. This will again reinforce the reliability of the business entity. These types of payments are traceable and you can ask for a charge back in case you are not satisfied with the genuineness of the supplier.

Most fraudulent online businesses ask for an advance payment, or payment via wire transfer or routing through money transfer channels like Western Union. Keep away from these types of businesses.

Another way to find out details of a supplier is to check the legal status of the business through government agencies like the Companies House website in UK and similar governmental sites in other countries. This will give you details about the status of the company, contact details, Sales Tax, VAT/ GST registration number etc.

Though proprietorship companies need not register with registrar of companies, but checking with the government authorities give you those important information, so that you don't waste your time and money. Better to be safer than repent later on.

You can also find out the details of the business from local Chambers of Commerce and Industry. Some businesses may not register with the chambers of commerce. However, someone there may be able to give you information about a particular trader or business under his or her jurisdiction.

As already indicated in the earlier pages, for physical shops, the best method of sourcing products for sales is the wholesaler/distributor channels. However, for a retailer to be more profitable and increase sales, has to go in for an online store along with his physical store.

Drop shipping is the only means of starting a new online business without investing a penny in stocks.
How it works?

You sell the product that you like at a   pre-determined price and when the customer buys your product, you collect payment and pay the drop shipper. The drop shipper delivers the goods to the customer.   The difference in the price is your profit. Drop shippers render the following services for you When you sold the product, the drop shipper fulfills your order on your instructions. The drop shipper packs your order and dispatches the goods direct to your customer.

The customer thinks that the stock has come direct from you. The drop shipper holds the stock and hence you do not have to lock your capital. There are few reliable, trusted and well-established drop shipping service providers. The names of drop shipping companies are given in the Essential Tools and Services chapter.

Tip No.4

When you buy from a verified wholesaler or drop shipper, you save lots of your time, avoid headaches and above all, your precious money and gets peace of mind. Look for logos like BBB (US only), TRUSTe, VeriSign, and SSL certificates with Extended Validation (EV), like the https://your domain.com in green (now a days instead of this most safe websites display a green lock before the https) *light with picture of the secure lock at the start.*

In addition, if the site is having a verified by Visa or MasterCard logo, it is most reliable. This may be rare, but if it is there well and good. Other signs to look for are D & B certified wholesaler and inspection done by Interteck, SGS or other highly reputed international inspection agencies.

Tip No.5

Before you start researching for products, find out a factory authorized wholesaler, who is willing to work with a small new retailer like you, preferably in your local area, district, state, or country. Remember that not all wholesalers may work with a newbie. However, it is essential to find a wholesaler who is willing to work with you. This will avoid a lot of headache and frustration when you start researching products to sell.

Making a Research List

Start compiling a wide range of products based on the niche you like to start and then narrow it down to the very specific product that can be sold online or offline, without much competition. However, doing it manually takes lots of your time and energy. Therefore, do not forget to use automation tools designed especially for this purpose.

You can start with products you like, then your family, then your friends and so on. From there, start compiling unrelated products, thereby you will be going away from traditional path and reach different categories of products that can sell without much difficulty. While doing your market research, you will come across many big sellers selling a product that is less than your purchase price.

My dear friend, don't get disheartened. The reason for a low selling price is that he/she may be buying in bulk because of which they get an additional volume discount. Hence, they are able to sell at lower rates. However, this should not stop you from researching low hanging fruits that you can sell at a higher profit.

Another important thing to remember is that doing manually all the research work is time consuming, tedious and sometimes frustrating. Therefore, it is better to use automation tools to minimize the efforts and save time and money. A list of the best tools is given in the Essential Tools and Services chapter.

Tip No.6

Remember that real wholesalers do not advertise in the search engines and their websites may not be very attractive, whereas fake entities do.

How and Where to find real Factory authorized wholesalers?

The best method is to wade through company websites and contact their sales department and through them the sales rep. In most cases, companies do not deal directly with a retailer, but occasionally you may come across a few. In case the answer from the sales department of the manufacturer is negative, ask the sales rep, he/she, whether they can recommend some authorized wholesaler s. This trick will work and you can get their authorized wholesaler's contact details like address, website, telephone number etc.

Working with Wholesale Suppliers

Now that you have researched and compiled the data you require starting your product identification. The next step is working with the wholesale suppliers. Similarly, as you have handled the manufacturer's rep, you need to call up the sales rep in the wholesaler's office for getting an account.

Certain etiquettes

For the first time when you are calling a wholesaler's rep, remember to call from a landline rather than a cell phone or smartphone. At times, the calls from cell phones are disturbing.

Second, be nice to receptionists. After all, they are also humans. If you are calling from home, switch off all the background sounds from TV, music systems and kids howling. The idea is to have a peaceful atmosphere. If you mention that you are a home based eBiz, sometimes you may not get a warm welcome.

However, do not worry; take it in its stride. Try to persuade the rep with your good mannerisms. If you got the right person and willing to provide you with an account, he or she may ask a few questions about your business like, business name, location, Tax ID, address, phone and fax number, business status like proprietorship, partnership or corporate, hours of business, trade reference and bank reference, license, number of years in business and so on.

She may also ask for details like estimated purchase from current wholesaler , product mix, size of customer base, physical store front, and D and B number (this is to ascertain about your credit worthiness), when starting out, this may not be an immediate requirement, but when you established your business, you may go for it.

The whole questions may be to know whether you are looking for the 30 days credit facility (known as Net 30). Therefore, please don't get scared, tell the rep that you are a new business and currently not looking for credit.

Dealing with Chinese Suppliers

Small retailers who sell on eBay and Amazon or on their own web site will be interested in getting products from Asia, in particular Chinese made items, which is cheaper, of good quality and supplier is dependable. When dealing with Chinese suppliers, it will be better if you engage a third party to deal with the supplier like an Agent or Trading Company, preferably from Hong Kong, where people speak better English than in other parts of China.

You need to have a Customs Broker and a freight forwarder, to take care of transportation/shipping for you. If you can find an agency does all the three jobs for you, well and good. There are a few highly reputed suppliers/traders, who do it for you. You can find out the details in the chapter dealing with Essential Tools and Services section of this book.

Handling Returns

Whether you know it or not, during the holiday season starting from October until January, the volume of business starts peaking and swells during November, December. Therefore, the amounts of returns are also high during the holiday season sales. There may not be any specific reason for the returns, but some buyers are unscrupulous during the holiday season as they enjoy the purchase during holiday season.

You must be prepared to deal with sales returns in your stride and cool your heals. However, you will notice that these few months give you maximum sales and profits too. Therefore, do not crap the few return sometime reaching a high of over 10%. However, the average return is in the range of 1% to 5%, which is common.

Believe me, the maximum sales returns are from the cell phone accessories followed by jewelry, consumer electronic, cameras and baby products. Therefore, it is better to select products that sell well e.g. specialized products, and have good margins.

Chapter 6

KEYWORD RESEARCH

Keyword research is one of the very important processes in identifying and promoting your product. First you have to identify the product, niche or micro niche. Then identify large number of keywords related to that niche or product.

There are three broad categories of phrases or words viz. broad match, phrase match and exact match. The exact match will help in assessing the short-term traffic potential, while phrase match gives the medium term traffic potential and broad match gives you the long-term traffic potential of a particular keyword or phrase.

There are four main steps involved in keyword research. They are: relevancy, traffic (not just traffic, but targeted traffic), competition and commerciality. Based on the niche or product you are promoting, you need to identify the theme keyword relevant to your product, niche, or a micro niche, e.g. "apparel".

It will be impossible to do the job of keyword research manually and the best thing is to use a keyword research tool like the free Google Keyword Planner. After getting a list of keywords, refine the keywords using some other keyword research software for getting results that are more accurate.

There are many tools available, each claiming the best in the market. However, I have done a thorough research and after using it I found the best tool, you can find the names of the same in the Essential Tools and Service chapter.

Using these tools, you can find out the most relevant keyword related to your product, how to price your product, your competition, demography and advertising used and business analytics, which you can use to improve and sell more, even competing with the big players in the marketplace.

The next step in keyword research is to identify the amount of traffic your selected keyword or phrase is getting in organic search both local and global searches monthly, for that particular keyword. This gives an idea about how many searchers are likely to visit your site and how many will purchase your product or service.

The third step in keyword research is to identify the competition in the market for that particular keyword and/or your niche/product. This gives you insight into the viability of your business. The fourth and final step in keyword research is to find out whether your niche or product will fetch you any profit.

The process of keyword research can be summed up in the following words. First, you will find a theme keyword, pertaining to a particular category or keyword, and thereafter the long tail derivative keyword and finally the semantic long tail keyword.

Long tail key word
Eg.
Apparel
Apparel for teenagers
Apparel for women
Apparel for women with blue borders

Long tail derivative keyword
E.g.
women's apparel

Theme keyword:
women's apparel
Long tail derivative keyword:
designer apparel for women

Semantic keyword:
Women's apparel nighty

The main advantage of long tail keywords are that they have low volume of traffic and lower competition and better chances of ranking in the organic search results. As such, long tail keywords do not generate volumes of traffic. Therefore, you will have to find out many such long tail key words related to your product to get volume.

To test how keyword research is done, just login with your Gmail account to Google, then start using Google Planner. They will ask you to verify your identity, then verify and you get permission to use the tools free.

Therefore, the secret to success is to identify highly relevant keywords that gets good traffic, competition is at an acceptable level and have high commerciality. Normally, the best relevant keywords searched by people are long tail keywords, also known as buyer keywords.

Traffic

As per the latest statistics, only 4 per cent traffic comes from search engines and rest 96 percent traffic comes from other sources. Therefore, just adjusting with SEO, alone will not get you the traffic you need to sell your product or service online. Therefore, what is the answer? It is, from other sources like Social Networks (about 65% from Facebook, Twitter, YouTube, Pinterest,

Wechat and Linkedin), blogs, article directories, video sites, newsletters, reciprocal links, etc.

You can get targeted traffic to your site using PPC, but it involves huge amount of money. In order to get the desired results, you need to use a judicious mix of traffic formulas including PPC. Above all, identify the phrases most relevant to the content on your site.

Competition

First, you must identify the level of competition a particular keyword or phrase related to your niche or product. This can be found out through the page ranking or search results i.e. the top ten results on the front page of Google.

The next thing is to ascertain the strength of competition i.e. how many people are competing for a keyword or phrase. Some are having low level of competition some keywords have high level of competition. Therefore, it is not advisable to compete with the very strong competitors i.e. web sites having many years of existence and is highly optimized. Therefore, in your own interest, please compete with lesser competitive web sites for keywords in your niche or product category so that there is a good chance of success and thereby more sales.

You might have noticed that the main reason for failure of an internet business is due to the failure of not assessing the strength of competition and without analyzing profitability and without any thought, create content. If the strength of the completion is too high, there is no chance of success. Therefore, pick your niche or keyword related to your product very carefully so that you do not have to repent later.

Commerciality

How do you know that the product or niche you have selected can succeed in the market place? In order to know the commercial value of the keyword or phrase related to your product or niche, the best thing to do is to find out the commerciality of the phrases you have selected. Commerciality means the profitability potential of a particular keyword or phrase. In order to know this, you need to pick high commercial value keywords with less competition. If you select a keyword or phrase, which is having low commercial value, then the chance of earning a good profit is minimal.

It will be a good idea to select a keyword or phrase having at least 50 daily visitors for that keyword and competition less than 100000 pages. How do you assess the strength of competition? By identifying the age of competing web site, page rank of the web site, back links to the web pages and ranking domains, back links from .edu and .gov domains, listing in Dmoz, Yahoo and Bing, web pages optimized with high ranking keywords in the title, URL, description and header tags.

Market Viability, Selection of products for your niche and assessment of market viability is another important and perhaps the last thing to do in your product selection process. Wrong selection of products and without assessing the market viability, will undo all your efforts and can have disastrous consequences. Most people have a belief that if an untapped niche or market is chosen, they can succeed. However, in reality, the truth is that it is always better to go with established and successful brands or products that will ensure profitability with lesser efforts and cost.

Tip No.7

If you are selling on Amazon, it is better to pick products with lesser sales rank. i.e. less competition.

Note

Keyword research must be an integral part of your business activity and it should be continuously and vigorously pursued. If necessary, you should use other tools for plucking profitable keywords of your competitors.

Further, if you are selling on eBay and Amazon, you must use specialized tools to know the profitability of your products before listing at eBay or Amazon. You can find names of a few such tools in the chapter dealing with essential tools and services.

Chapter 7

WEB DESIGN, CONTENT AND OPTIMIZATION

This Chapter deals with one of the most important aspects related to starting your new online internet based small business. Therefore, attention must be given to important aspects, while designing the web pages.

Web Page Design

Most shopping cart providers offer free web page templates and web site builder software, which did not require any programming skills and comes as Do It Yourself (DIY) package. However, it will be a good idea, if affordable, buy special and exclusive themes or templates, especially with the latest features like HTML5, CSS3 and Responsive (responsive web pages will work seamlessly on all devices like desktop, laptop, mobile and tablets). This will give you an advantage and separate you from the crowd.

In addition to detailed description and high resolution images of your product, don't forget to include all your store details like, about us, contact address, phone number , email, FAQ, hours of work, live chat agent, terms of service, privacy policy, site map, link to social media like Face book, Twitter, Linkedin, Pinterest, Google+, You Tube and RSS feed for blog.

The web pages should not have any clutter, give lots of white space so that when a customer land on your web site, it gives a pleasant look and feeling of comfort for the visitor. Therefore, select themes, which are clean and pleasant to the eyes. If affordable, it will be a nice idea to include the Zoom Plus feature or the 360° zoom feature for your product images. However, this will cost you some extra bucks, but it is worth the money.

If you are selling on Flipkart or Amazon and other reputed platforms you get this feature free of cost as part of listing with them.

In addition, don't forget to provide the sliding Live Chat screen (preferably from the upper right hand corner i.e. at eye level). This will help the visitor to spend more time on your web page and can help her to take a purchase decision.

Mobile and Tablet Enabled Web Pages

While designing and/or selecting your web site design or readymade shopping carts, as the case may be, do not forget to enable your web pages compatible with Mobile and Tablets. As the mobile market is going to be the future, more are more people are using smart phones and tablets for interaction and information gathering as well as purchase goods using mobile commerce feature.

It is highly recommended to go in for a web site that is compatible with any kind of browsing, viz. desktop, mobile or tablet including tiny phones and retina devises that too with a single URL instead of different URLs like dotcom, dot m, or dot mobi. This will avoid unnecessary redirects, better search results and increase customer retention. Hence, please use Responsive templates or themes.

Optimize your images dynamically to fit all types of screen sizes and resolutions. This will dramatically reduce page load times and increase user engagement, accelerate performance of asset rendering in responsive websites, and reduce bandwidth costs and result in a better bottom line for your business.

Once you selected the template and other features that you would like to include in your page design, start incorporating the content with sufficient amount of keyword spread in your item description, but do not overdo it. Restrict the keyword spread to 1 - 1.5 percent. Give lot of white spaces; do not clutter your web pages with more stuff. Give breathing space to the visitor.

For a beautiful web site, look at the web pages of IBM.com

As regards write up, don't give more than 500 words per page. It will be ideal if the content is restricted to 300-350 words per page. Use high definition digital quality pictures of your products. Use anchor texts in your product graphic description e.g. Designer Shoes f or women using a HTML code like this:
<a href="http://www.example.com/">Designer Shoes for Women</a> [replace with your domain name and keyword]

Warning

Don't overdo this, otherwise, Google will punish you since Google wants you to follow good practices and encourage quality and originality of contents and hence restrict the usage of Hyper Text Links. You can use it in your Headings and a few other places in the Article and send the visitor to your Home Page or other specific pages that are relevant to the anchor keyword. Just because you created a web store do not expect that you will get lots of traffic (visitors) and sales. This is a misconception.

As running a brick and mortar shop, in internet based online business too, there are certain important aspects need to be adhered to get the desired results. They are:

Search Engine Optimization (SEO) Why do you want to optimize your web pages? Because, people search for products and services on the internet using search engines. More than 1.2 trillion searches are made daily in Google alone for information.

They have money and they come there to buy products or services. 75 percent of searchers never look farther than page one, hence if you get a ranking of 11 i.e. on the second page, many searchers do not even have any idea about your web site, unless she venture out and look at the second page of search results. With over 4 billion web pages on the internet, getting a front-page ranking in Google search is almost impossible, but not difficult with certain techniques.

Since Google is the undisputed leader among search engines with over 77 percent market share, optimizing your web pages with high ranking and most relevant keywords is necessary.

Search engines use various criteria in ranking your pages like Latent Semantic Indexing (LSI) or popularly known as algorithms, age of the web site, hypertext matching, back links from other web pages, internal linking structure, keyword density, domain age etc.

In order to get the top ranking in organic searches, your web pages must have certain important ingredients like; back links from high page ranking web sites and that must be timely and relevant to your page content. In addition, you must have well optimized and original content pages with 1 to 1.5 percent keyword density, not only on the headings, but also in content as well. Google uses the hypertext-matching feature to scan your web pages. Again, for getting top ranking on front page of search engines like Google, you need to have more pages on your site. The more the merrier.

How do people find your web site?

To get the top 10 of the search results, i.e. first page of Google, Yahoo or Bing. Not all the web pages get the top ranking. Only the most relevant keyword optimized web pages can get top rankings. In addition, it takes lot of time, the least case about 2-3 months.

There are other factors like, internal and external linking, internal page linking, and site map, back links from highly relevant and top ranking web sites like educational and government web sites, related to your product.

Note: *If you are planning to get a web site designed by a third party, opt for reputed players like Amazon AWS, Google channel partners and the reputed shopping cart providers, who have many service providers approved and listed on their web site.*

Use of Buyer Keywords

Normally, when for the first time, people search the web using a particular keyword or phrase, basically for information about a product or service that they are interested in. This type of keywords will have huge search volumes. It is unlikely that this type of searchers buy something.

Hence, you may not get any kind of result by optimizing your pages with broad category keywords.

E.g.
Software,
Cameras,
Shoes,
Apparel

In the second phase of search, people do it for comparison. The searcher now knows what she wants. Therefore, the search will be around a specific keyword.

E.g.
Apparel for women
Mp3 player 8 GB
Mp3 player under $100
Acme mp3 player

People who use keywords for comparing are more ready to buy. Comparing keywords are probably the best keywords that you can target for your search engine optimization campaign. They often have much lower search volume than general keywords but they will lead to more sales and it is much easier to get top 10 rankings for these keywords.

The third phase of search is for buying. Here they are looking for the web site with the best price, quality and service. For these reasons, they use very specific keywords (known as buyer keywords) for searches, in particular, long tail keywords.

E.g.
Acme 3Beat move 8 GB Video MP3 Player
Acme 3Beat move 8 GB free shipping
Example Corp. Megaplayer Clip 1 GB

People who use buying keywords are ready to buy. However, remember that if you use competing keywords, you will not get much advantage. The best keywords for search engine optimization are the comparing keywords, because, people who use these keywords for comparison are looking for a solution to their problems.

Tip No.8

For getting better ranking, do not use single keywords, instead use, multiple keywords, or long tail keywords, most relevant to your product.

After identifying, the most relevant and high-ranking keywords, with less competition, optimize the web pages using the keywords. If any of your web pages are already ranking, do not make any changes.

How to Get High Page Ranks

Do not use Frames; avoid Flash and other multimedia elements. Do not use welcome page, choose reliable and fast hosting service like a cloud hosting. For a good ecommerce site, you need to have over 150 GB band widths if your page views are high. Please do not use a shared hosting plan for your ecommerce site instead use only exclusive ecommerce hosting platform, in case you cannot afford cloud hosting in the beginning.

Also, check the HTML code of your web pages, do not try to trick using black hat or other techniques, and do not use re-directs. Please ensure that your web site can be crawled by search engines by properly configuring the robots.txt file.

Please ensure that search engines can spider your web pages. So ensure that enough text is there in your web pages. In images, use the <Image Alt> texts.

Use the correct http status code. Do not forget to resolve any DNS issues before submitting it for search engine spidering, as it takes an average 2-4 days time to get your Domain Name pointed to the server.

Another important thing to remember is to have sufficient original content in your web pages. Please do not use recycled, or PLR content on your web site.

Link Building

Link building is another important factor influencing the ranking of your web site in searches. There are two types of links viz. inbound links and outbound links. Inbound links or back links from high-ranking sites relevant to your product or niche can help you rank high in search results. However, remember that the back links should not have a No Follow attribute. Get only Do Follow links from other most relevant web sites.

Similarly, links from high authority sites relevant to your web pages, like education or Government web sites, can also help your site rank high. Also, remember that getting good links from relevant sites are good, but do not overdo it. Sometimes, it will be tempting to hurry and get some links from irrelevant sites and also using automated link building tools, link exchanges etc. are not advisable.

Tip No.9

While attempting to build back links, please use one word keywords relevant to your web site, means broad phrase or keyword e.g. 'Camera' instead of too specific keywords, like long tail keywords. In addition, use links from Blogs.

There are millions of blogs on the Internet and they all need something to write about. Getting links from blogs is a good way to get links from related websites. How to Improve your Link Building Efforts

It is not that easy to get good links from relevant web pages related to your product or niche. But done properly, it can improve your site rankings in search results. Here are a few tips to improve link-building efforts.

Don't require much action from the web master
Don't try to teach other web masters about SEO
Keep your email message short and crisp
Don't ask for a link if the other web site is not r elated to your niche or topic.
Take the initiative to link to the web site first.
Ensure that your web site has professional look and neat design.
Be polite and humble
Avoid free emails (like @gmail.com, @yahoo.com etc, instead use a private, email e.g. email@yourdomain.com
Provide full contact information. Offer an incentive to link back to your web site.

How to Convert Visitors into Buyers

Web surfers hate to wait for slow loading web pages. All you get is a maximum of 8 seconds. If your web pages don't load fast enough, many web surfers will go away without taking a look at them.

No matter how great your product is if your website is not fast enough, web surfers will not see it. Fast loading web pages are crucial if you want to sell something on the Internet. First and foremost in getting faster loading time is to ensure that your web site is hosted with a reliable fast server.

The following steps will ensure faster loading.
Reduce number of graphics.

Specify the dimensions of your image i.e. width and height.

Make the top of your web page something interesting.

Use CSS to divide your tables.

Double check cell widths

Create Trust

Ensure that your web pages have a simple but professional design.

Tell your visitors who you are i.e. create an about us page.
Offer free trials, if possible, and show your refund policy.
Use testimonials in your web pages.

Use the Right Words to Increase Sales

What is in it for your customers?

Do not mix up features and benefits. Customers are more interested in knowing what benefit she will get from buying your product. Therefore, provide accurate and useful information about your product or service.

Use Attention Grabbing Headlines

Your headlines should make clear what to expect in the next sentences and they should grab your visitors' attention.

Use words like free, proven, benefit, first, discover, complete, exclusive, and avoid words like should, could, or but.
Make sure that you use you more than I or we. Remember: Your customers do not really care about you and your business. They only want to know what is in it for them.
Finish your sales copy by telling the reader what to do, i.e. a strong call-to-action:

e.g. "Click here to buy Gucci designer shoes"
Optimize your Order Pages

Statistics show that more than 60 percent of online shoppers abort the ordering process. If your order page is not easy to use, all other website promotion efforts will be in vain.

Most important points for a successful order page

Link from the home page and from all product and service pages to the order page.

Give the links on your order page names that your customers can easily recognize: "Order", "Buy", "Store", "Checkout", etc.

Don't hide the price for your products or services. People will not buy if they do not know what they have to pay.

Tell your visitors about shipping costs and state taxes.
Tell your visitors the final price before they have to enter the credit card number.

Tell your visitors who you are and tell them your complete company address, contact phone number, email address, and provide live chat facility, or a toll-free number, if possible.

Offer an unconditional money-back guarantee, if possible.
Tell your visitors upfront about your refund policy.

Make sure that your order pages are secure so that your customers can safely enter their contact and purchase information.

Make sure that your order pages are easy to understand.

Test them with your friends or relatives, who do not connect to the Internet very often.

Regularly test your order pages to make sure that they work well.
Make sure that you will be notified, in case your server goes down.

Ensure that your order page displays a meaningful message if the customer forgets to enter the street name or any other required field.

Make sure that your order pages work with international customers. Some customers don't know what to enter in the "State" field and usually leave it empty.

Some countries don't even have postal numbers. Your order pages should work for these customers.

Professional Look

If your order pages are easy to use and secure, they will not hinder or deter customers from completing their purchase. Don't forget to give as much secure a site as possible by providing the SSL Certificate on your site page.

Most shopping cart/payment gateways offer a 128-bit SSL and some the 256 bit extended validation i.e. with the secure lock and https://www.yourdomain.com displayed in green.

Before optimizing your web page, finding the most relevant, and top-notch keywords related to your product or niche, is of great importance in getting a first page ranking in search results. A wrong keyword can spoil your entire effort.

In addition, it will be great waste of time, money, and efforts. It is impossible to do every aspect of search engine optimization manually. Therefore, using specific automation tools like SEO, Keyword research, back link building, search engine submission, page rank checker etc is necessary.

These tools does all the job for you, like identifying the top notch key words related to your niche or product, web page optimization, competition analysis, finding their keywords, URL, Title and Header tags, keyword spread and so on. You can find the details in the essential tools and services chapter.

How to get more Sales out of your Web Store?

There are certain factors influencing the sale of products on your web store. These are true for any type of store whether it is in auction sites like eBay or fixed price listing like Amazon.

eBay

If you are selling on eBay auctions, experiment with different formats like fixed price listing as different types of inventory sell well in certain categories and format. Therefore, experimenting will be a good idea to get more sales. Write winning titles and descriptions. Accurate information about your product including keyword rich title e.g. 'instead of just "Camera" title your product with long tail keywords "buy Canon Digital SLR Camera DQ5000". This will distinguish your product with other sellers, since customer finds your product as per their interest and buy from your store.

Adding high definition images of your Product enhances the chances of a sale manifold and the prospective buyer can see the product in fr ont of their eyes, take a faster decision about buying it. Take pictures with a clear background and from different angles. You can add up to 12 pictures in eBay. Use the zoom and enlarge facilities. This is especially useful when marketing through mobile devices.

Get top rated seller status by offering 14 days or more, return policy. In places like eBay, there is cutthroat competition. Therefore, it is essential to price your products competitively.

A normal pricing strategy can be as follows:

Cost of product + drop ship fee + merchant account transaction fee. To this, add cost of transportation, for getting the items from your supplier i.e, Light Bulk Wholesalers.

Then look for competitors and set your price after adding all your input costs and reasonable profit margins. Ideally a 10-15 percent margin is quite a good profit on eBay.

Do not price your products too high, or too low. Open small focused internet stores. Use Drop shipping. Stick with one wholesaler for each product category. Use UPS, FedEx, DHL, or such other highly reputed and reliable transporters for shipping. There may be separate handling charges for drop shipping.

There are various techniques that you can use to enhance sale of your products, viz. offering free shipping, e.g. club a few items and offer the buyer the free shipping facility, if the customers buys from you, immediately. Alternatively, you can offer an expedited shipping i.e. one day shipping.

Listing your products with item specifics and attributes or customizing them. Item specifics let you provide details about the item you are selling, such as brand, size, type, color, and style.

Using the best offer facility, which is free, eBay will list your product in the best offer category and expose your product in front of more prospective buyers. The trick is offer a little discounted price. This way you increase the sales numbers and thereby your profitability. This technique will be most suited for fixed price listings.

In auction type of sales, there may be a prospective buyer who is looking for instant gratifications i.e. buy immediately. Therefore, by offering a 'Buy Now Button' in your auction price listing can increase your sales. If you are listing different variations of a product, e.g. black shoes, white ribbon etc., put all these in one listing at one place. This will increase your visibility and get more sales.

Prime Reasons for the Failure of a Business

Most businesses fail within the first three months of starting the business. The major reasons for the failure are no planning, no market research, or survey, improper selection of products, and market segmentation. According to a recent online research study report, 56 percent of web sites have no street address. 90 per cent have no maps, 44 per cent have no phone number, 78 per cent does not have an email address provided on their web site. Another 96 percent have no Facebook or Twitter links.

When it comes to Shopping Carts on the web site, in as much as 98 percent have no spam protection, 76 percent have no privacy policy, and 89 percent have no video on their site. These are all very important aspects of running a successful online business.

In addition, there are startling revelations by the above online research, 87 percent web sites have no Facebook pages, 94 percent have no YouTube presence, 97 per cent have no Linkedin presence, 98 per cent have no Google+ presence, and 92 percent have no blog on their site. It is even astonishing to find that 98 percent of web sites are not mobile optimized. Most of the web sites have less number of pages, whereas the thump rule is to have more information on the web site. Similarly, the time taken to load the page is very high. This will result in visitors leaving the site without even looking at the site. Therefore, rectify this flaw by testing your sites before submitting to Search Engines.

Finally, the most important flaw in web site design is not giving proper attention to SEO factors. Seventy-four percent sites have no location in Meta title, 95 percent sites have duplicate contents, which Google finds spamming, and another 24 percent sites have no or zero page rank, which results in no result in organic search results and 97 percent people do not use micro-formats, which can help the site in getting Google's rich snippets.

Therefore, giving adequate time in design of your site is necessary, because getting highly targeted traffic to your site is necessary to get the green bucks, I mean a decent sale. So don't be carried away by the packaged shopping cart solution provider's tall claims, test it and do your due diligence before finalizing a deal with them for your web store.

Some of the important points to remember while designing your web pages are: About us page, navigation buttons, privacy policy, contact us, terms of service, refund policy, FAQ, toll free number or telephone number, name and address, email, live chat agent, ticketing system etc.

In addition, browser testing is necessary for both desktop/notebook and mobile versions of your site. *Compulsorily do an A/B or split test and multi* variant testing (especially with images) to ensure that you are not wasting money on a new web site, which is not profitable.

A well optimized with SEO, HTML5, CSS3 and Responsive Template or Theme can take care of this. Split testing will give you the information that you need, like which keywords, phrases, images or a combination of all these works best for you, so that you can make the necessary changes including the domain name, ad captions, and content.

How to get Top Ranking in Local Searches

Your website is listed in Google's local results depends on several factors, like the location of your business, the industry that you are in, the keywords that you are targeting, and other things influence your listing in Google Places. Therefore, if you are a local business, it is highly advisable to include your business name and place name in your domain e.g.,www.FreshBakersVictoria.com or www.drGibbsDentalLosangeles.com.

Some of the important tips to get top local page ranking is to have a local business address, list your business in the appropriate category, and include best key words in your business name, mention or list your business in free local yellow pages (by doing this you get citation of your business as reference), craigslist etc.

This enhances the reputation of your business and Google think that your business is real. In addition, your business name, address and phone number has to be consistent across the different websites that list your business.

Get recommendations, positive reviews and ratings from viewers. This will help Google to gain more confidence in your web site. The more positive reviews your web site has, the better. Encourage your customers to write a positive review, if they are satisfied with your product or service.

Another factor influencing the ranking of your web pages in local list is the proximity to the searched location. Thus adhering to these aspects can give you good responses and thereby increase your business.

Yet another important matter needs your attention is the correct use of HTML codes. Therefore, don't forget to validate your site using W3C validation tool. You can check it out the same at http://www.w3schools.com, and select the appropriate W3C validator tool from the menu and correct the mistakes, if any.

Based on customer demand, you can create a product or modify the one you already have or alternatively, find the exact product from elsewhere so that you can encash on the public demand. Surveys will also enable you to get highly targeted customer list from the respondents.

Online Surveys

Using online surveys gives you very important insights into promoting and marketing products that sells. You get the information regarding what the people are interested in. Don't guess; find out from the public what they are really looking for. If done properly, surveys will give you great marketing intelligence. It saves your time, money, efforts and increases your Return on Energy (RoE).

Imagine that you want to sell a particular product with certain type of benefits and features, then through the online survey you found out that this is not the product people are looking for, instead they want something different. Therefore, surveys can reveal what the customer thinks about a particular product.

Conducting Surveys

Send emails to a group from your list. If no list, try through jv partners list. Otherwise, run a survey using any email-marketing agency or specialized survey companies, and send survey questions to the opt-in list i.e. a landing page specially designed for this purpose. A list of such companies names are available in the chapter dealing with Essential Tools and Services.

Alternatively, you can request moderators of discussion groups or news groups to take a survey. Then opt for the auto responder service to collect emails and then send the questions to them.

If necessary, ask for their opinion as well, in a few lines. Make top of the page very interesting so that visitors can hang around for a while.

Use testimonials, show benefits, don't use technical jargons, use small paragraphs with headings for each paragraph, end your sales copy with a strong call-to-action "Buy now and get an extra discount of e.g. $5".

Tip No.10

Please note that instead of a percentage discount, mention monetary value because the customer is not interested in knowing the percentage, but want to know the exact amount she will be saving. Optimize your order pages and list details like, price, taxes, shipment cost, delivery, and warranty.

Chapter 8

MARKETING AND PROMOTION

Once you have finished your research and analysis, finalized the product(s) that you wish to promote, the next step will be to decide about mode of operation. Do you want to sell direct to customers through your own web site or would you like to sell the product(s) through an established third party platform like Amazon or eBay.

As I have already mentioned in the introduction chapter, it is always better to start with an already established or in demand product that has lot of buyers for it, because you need not do anything for promoting and establishing the product in the market. If you are planning to sell a physical product, Amazon is the best place to start with. When you have learned the art of online selling and gained mastery over it, you can proceed with other venues like eBay and further into your own web store. However, if you are an already experienced person, know everything about selling online, then, you can proceed with creating your own independent web store.

Note

If you have local shop, say limited to certain area, city and so on, then it will be beneficial to have a web site listed locally and do your promotion through various media viz. Radio, glow sign boards, local newspaper ads, specialized magazines in your area, even dropping a pamphlet through news papers is also a good idea, that too periodically, say once in a month or once in three months etc.

In this fast paced world, there is no need to go in for designing a web site through some costly web designers and then buy each and every item required for the store to get from different sources.

These include domain name, web hosting, shopping cart, and payment gateway, promotional and analytical tools. Well-established and popular selling platforms like Amazon, eBay, Flipkart etc. provide an all-in-one solution for starting your online store. All you have to do is to get the product details, images, pricing, shipping information and then list your products using their easy to use tools. In a few hours and you are ready to sell your products online.

Tip No.11

Start selling one product at a time, low priced and low competition. When you start earning profits, increase the number of products and to high value, then go in for more and more products in your niche or niches. Duplicate your successes in one niche to similar other product or niche.

However, don't put your foot in several baskets at a time till such time you gain valuable experience in online selling. Going forward, you may need several tools for running your business more efficiently. I have given the list separately in a chapter dealing with Essential Tools and Services needed for a successful online business. These are very efficient and handy tools and services, which will reduce your time and effort and enhance your profitability.

Browser Testing

Before doing anything, please test your web pages for browser flaws. Using web browsers like, Google, Yahoo, AOL, Bing (MSN), Firefox or Opera. You can do the testing by yourself both for desktop/notebook and mobile, to know flaws, if any, so that you do not get embarrassed after going live. The best way to do this is to request your family members, friends, or relatives to do it. Only thing is that you do not tell them why you are doing this test.

Just tell them to check it up to get their opinion. While doing so, stay closely and look for flaws so that you can make note of any flaws that requires correction.

Split Testing

The next thing to do is to do A/B testing known as split testing, and multivariate testing using images to ascertain, which keywords or phrases, what type of image gives the best results in searches. Split testing will give you exact information about what works best for you and which option gives you the best results so that you can concentrate on that aspects before submitting your web site. The best way to conduct split testing is by using a landing page with strong call- to-action.

How to do AB Testing/Split Testing of your Landing Page?

When it comes to spit testing, there is always a big dilemma about what elements should be tested for identifying the best response rate? Here are the four most important elements that you must test for, especially on a landing page.

The Offer

Start your optimization process by identifying what types of offers convert the most visitors into leads, and which offers help you push leads down the sales funnel. It is found that e-books get better response than webinars in converting visitors to leads. However, webinars do better than e-books in converting leads to customers. Therefore maintaining a balanced mix of content is necessary.

You may also test different topics and find out how they compare at driving business results by doing a split test promotion of two topics to a single email list, and see which topic generates more conversions.

The Description

People looking for information online will pay attention to the description of your offer on the landing page. Experiment with different landing page copy to help you drive more conversions. For instance, bullet points and data-driven content have traditionally performed well.

Start with a radical test in which you compare a short, one-paragraph long description to longer, but still valuable copy to determine which kind of content works best for your audience.

Form Fields

Landing page A/B testing enables you to evaluate how your audience reacts to different questions what prospects are willing to answer and what information they would rather not share. Form fields help you qualify leads and nurture them.

Whatever content you gate, make sure to minimize the friction in your forms. To maximize conversions, keep the number of fields between three and seven. For dramatic results, consider a whole page redesign - where you A/B test two separate pages. It needs lot of efforts to come up with two designs, but this kind of test will improve your conversion rates.

Whole page tests can compare overall image placement, form length, and copy. Once you have statistically significant results pointing to the variation that performed better, you can continue optimizing through smaller tweaks.

Some other important aspects that you can use for testing the whole page is the head line, form field names, form button color, form button size, form button copy, for m headline, image, captions on image, copy and headline font size, use of video, use of social follow buttons, use of testimonials and use of third party seals of approval. Shopping Engines or Comparison Sites.

The next important place you should submit your web store or web site is in most popular shopping engines known as shopping comparison sites. Submit your site to as many shopping engines as possible. Properly formatted product feeds to shopping engines will result in better exposure for your products in the end. There are many shopping engines; they vary in size, specialty and shape.

Your product may perform well in some and some others not. Therefore, submit your product feeds and web site to as many shopping engines as possible, including the top one i.e. Google shopping, to get the maximum mileage out of it, based on your promo budget. The list of the most popular shopping engine names are given in the Essential Tools and Services chapter .

Shopping feeds are great for getting visibility. However, getting a sale from these sources is a different thing, as they mostly depend on the pricing, shipping and photo quality and so on. However, the main benefit is getting exposure for your store, especially from the paid listings.

Photo quality plays an important factor in getting visitors to your site and making a purchase decision. According to the standard rule, image size should be of 400 x 400 pixels, and they must be in the same domain and host.

Another factor influencing purchase decision is the freshness of the product feed with accurate product information, price details and availability. This plays an important role in sales particularly during peak seasons and highly competitive market.

Yet again, another important factor influencing more targeted visitors to your web store and thereby enhancing the sale of your product is through proper use of keywords, especially buyer keywords, in your shopping feeds.

A combined strategy of paid search (PPC/CPC), shopping feeds, SEO, and email marketing can result in more targeted visitors to your store and enhanced sales.

Apps for Mobile and Tablets

Since the mobile and tablet user numbers has increased substantially and now they are the largest access devise in the world of ecommerce especially Smart phones and Tablets over taking the domain from Desktops. Therefore, it will be in your own interest to develop apps featuring your products for mobile and tablet users. With the apps, you can get new customers, welcome your customers, increase engagements, conversions, and retain your customers with mobile.

Social Media Networks

Most businesses across the world increasingly use social media for interacting with prospects and customers to gain more and more foot hold in the market, gaining brand image and recommendations. Social media like Facebook, and FB Messenger, Google Plus, Twitter, Linkedin, YouTube, Pinterest, and now Whatsapp and WeChat has become so popular with people. Therefore, no one can ignore the importance of social media as a marketing tool.

Submission to Search Engines Directories for Indexing

Once everything is finished, and then it is time to submit your website to most popular search engines Google, Yahoo, Bing, and search directories like DMOZ, Yahoo and specialized shopping engines.

A list of specialized shopping engines is available in the essential Tools and Services chapter . Most search engine listings are free. However , Yahoo, charges an annual fee for commerce sites.

What is next?

You have identified your niche and products to promote, the selling platform i.e. storefront, payment gateway, shopping cart, and all the stuffs needed to sell your product online including spilt testing and browser testing.

Promoting Your Store

The next big step is to promote and sell your products through the select platform/market place, i.e. Amazon, eBay or your own web store. Whatever platform from you are selling your products, it is utmost important to know how to bring prospective buyer s to your store. Like the brick and mortar shop, location and traffic to your store is very essential to result in a sale.

Normally, if your shop is located in a prominent place in your city, it will be easy for customer s to reach your store. In cyber space, there are billions of web pages out there. Then how can a prospective buyer reach your store? Unless people know about your store and products you sell, no one will come to buy your products.

Therefore, you must promote your store in the online world to get visibility and brand awareness. Are you familiar with product promotion or promoting your store? If not, what is the alternative? Either you do it yourself or get it done through a third party. My dear friend, don't take it into heart. My job is to help you find various avenues to promote your store; through the best channels and help, you succeed in your venture.

A recent survey shows that only 4 percent traffic comes from the search engines and the rest 96 percent comes from other sources like popular web sites, ezines, article directories, blogging platforms, newsletters etc.

However, this 4 percent traffic itself is huge, considering the volume of online searches. Out of this, about 77 percent traffic comes from Google alone and the rest from Yahoo, Bing (MSN), and other specialized search engines. If you are targeting Chinese markets, then listing with Baidu is good option and they are now bigger than Yahoo.

Role of Social Networks

As already mentioned, if there is no visitors to your store, then, there will not be any sales, and the result is no income. Therefore, social networks play an important role in generating business through face-to-face interaction. Some of the important channels you must utilize to promote your store are:

Facebook

I don't think there is any need for an explanation about facebook as it is the most popular social media site with over 1871 million users. They have various interaction tools like a personal fan page, business page, groups, messenger etc. You can even create a copy of your web store in Facebook and sell products from there.

Facebook for Business

You can create a Facebook business page and use it for promoting your business in many ways. You can include updates, photos, videos and questions, page timeline, reach and engage your audience on the web and on mobile, and respond to people in a quick, more personal way.

News Feeds

Your Page is where you create posts that get shown in the news feed, the center of the Facebook experience. Newsfeed is where people spend their time on Facebook in fact, 40 percent. It's where people share their time, most important parts of their lives and where businesses can engage them in conversation.

According to Facebook's own words , successful posts are short - Posts between 100 and 250 characters get about 60% more likes, comments and shares. Visual - Photo albums, pictures, and videos get 180%, 120%, and 100% more engagement respectively. Optimized - Page Insights help you learn things such as what times people engage most with your content so you can post during those hours. Facebook advices its users to invite your influencers like family, friends and even employees to like your page.

As per the latest research statistics, the shares of social media channels are as follows: Facebook 86 percent, Googe+ 68 percent, LinkedIn 43 percent, Twitter 41 percent, Pinterest 29 percent and You Tube 25 percent.

Facebook Exchange

Another important feature of Facebook for business promotion is the Facebook Exchange, which comes under the paid category. Therefore, don't forget to use Facebook's paid programs especially their advertising program and their Power Editing feature in the Ad Manager.

Later on additional functions like create custom audiences, new lookalike audiences, retargeting, ecommerce conversion analytics, and partner categories added. Therefore, it becomes increasingly clear that major social media like Facebook, Twitter, Linkedin, Google+, Pinterest, YouTube, Flickr , Living Social, Stumpleupon and similar other channels can give you tremendous amount of publicity and branding at minimal cost, sometimes even without spending a dime.

WhatsApp and Messenger App

This important and very creative, piece of application is a revolutionary acquisition by Facebook, paying a whooping $19 billion. It has over 1300 million users. Very shortly, they will be coming out with a business version of Whatsapp.

As in September 2017, Facebook has 2061 million user base, WhatsApp and Facebook Messenger App has a combined user strength of over 2600 million. Therefore, this media is a very important channel for your business and use it wisely.

Twitter

Twitter is an online social networking and micro-blogging platform that enables its users to send and read text-based messages of up to 140 characters, known as "tweets". This limit of 140 characters may be increased to 250 shortly. They have a membership of over 328 million as of 2017 and a daily tweet of over 500 million. You can do a lot with 140 characters and can include videos and photos. It is an easy way to bring you closer to the people and topics you care about. It is necessary to have channel for any marketer for social engagement.

Linked In

With over 106 million members, it is the largest exclusive technical professionals' social media site. They also own Slide Share, which is the largest slide- sharing platform. In Linkedin, you can create your personal/business page, groups and use their paid advertising program to get targeted traffic to your site.

Google+

Google plus is the alternative to Face Book. With a fan following of over 219 Million, it is an immediate choice for any marketer to gain foothold and brand building.

Pinterest

Pinterest is a tool for collecting and organizing thing s you love. It is mainly for social interaction site where you can pin your web pages and link to your site. When people see your pages, they like it, then they can pin it to their page and their fan following and so on. You can use Pinterest for personal or business purpose. It has an active user base of 200 million.

There are many other social media and social networking sites, like WeChat, Tumblr, QQ, Instagram, Telegram, Diggit, Stumpleupon and so on. If you are in consumer product business, use Facebook, Twitter and YouTube to promote your business. In addition, you can use Pinterest and Google Plus for the same purpose. However, if your business is in Technical products or services category, then use LinkedIn, Facebook and YouTube combination in addition to Googleplus and Pinterest.

If used properly, this will give you maximum results for your business.

Note

Though you get more responses through the organic searches, it is increasingly evident that combined with paid promotions using Facebook, Twitter, LinkedIn, YouTube and Google Plus gives you more responses and thereby increases your return on investment RoI). I, therefore, strongly recommend, making use of Paid Promotions along with your organic efforts.

It is important to note that most market platform or selling channels like Flipkart, eBay, Amazon and most other leading players in the online space, has a paid advertising scheme. If you are listed in Amazon and other leading carts, pl use their paid ads as they have huge volume of traffic and they display first the products which are advertised with them. Now a days they are showing this information by mentioning sponsored product (i.e. ad) on the screen like the Google Ads.

Regarding how to set up a business page and use social networks like Facebook, Twitter, Google+, Pinterest, YouTube etc., you can get complete information, and guidance from their web sites. Just go to their home page, click on the "how to use......for Business" button, lo you are presented with enormous amount of information, that you can leverage for growing your business.

Very Important Tip

While using social media for lead generation, please take advantage of the 10+4+1 formula i.e. using content curation. Content curation involves searching, discovering, editorializing, and publishing others content on your social posts, which are relevant, timely, and useful.

The 10+4+1 formula is used like this: for every 15 social media post use 10 posts of others, 4 posts must be your own , and One original post of yours must lead to the landing page, where you offer incentives to collect customer information such as name, email, phone number or location and other details. This method will improve your conversion rates.

Press Releases

Press Releases, if used correctly, can give you tremendous amount of publicity and branding at a very nominal cost. This media must be utilized at least four to five times while starting your new business and thereafter, twice a month, or least case once a month. In addition, promote your site through press releases whenever there is a special promotion scheme like discount coupons, package deals etc. Press releases may not give you immediate business; however, it will give you a back link and send targeted traffic to your site.

There are various inter nationally reputed online PR agencies to do this job. They send your news to major search engines and are able to distribute your press releases to journalists and bloggers. They can deliver it to opt in news subscribers and host your news release on their web site for future reference.

The cost of a press release varies from $50 to $499 for a single press release. There are many free press release agencies, which can be utilized to get that extra mileage. However, they may not be as effective as the paid services; because they give primacy to paid service over free service and hence responses may be less.

The success of a press release depends upon the following factors, viz.

The Form

Your headline must be brief, comprehensive, and attention grabbing. The optional sub-heading, date line, the opening paragraph, body paragraph, contact information, call-to-action, writing and addressing in third person, all these must be written in clear conscience language.

Also, include your most important keywords, in your title and summary, proofread for grammar, punctuation, spelling mistakes, consistency and usage, anchor text and URL links configuration.

The content size must be about 300 - 500 words and properly mention trademark, company or product name consistently.

Promote your press release using social networks, relevant to your niche or product.

The Style

You must avoid sensationalism, gimmick, and cuteness. Your quotes must add human element and relevance and avoid outrageous claims in your press release. Properly document and substantiate everything before releasing.

The Images

A picture conveys a message thousand times better and generates faster recollection in the minds of the people. Hence, you must include images in your press release. Many people don't do this, which is a grave mistake. You can include your company logo, product image, web site screenshot, or your headshot.

Please ensure that nothing is offensive for your audience. Clearly mention the source of the news or press release, e.g. your company name, not that of xyz. Focus on main points and avoids irrelevant details. You must also check for legal issues, public companies, or celebrities and comply with press release standards.

I have given the names of the most reputed paid and free press release firms in the Essential Tools and Services chapter.

Affiliate Marketing

One of the zero cost marketing channels is affiliate marketing. Based on the product range you deal with, and the maximum commission you can offer to an affiliate, this will send targeted buyers to your web site, without spending a dime from your pocket. Since all the labor including promotion of your web site is did by the affiliates, this option must have a prominent place in your marketing strategy.

Normally, on physical products the commission varies from 4 percent to 20 percent. There will be people interested in sending customers to your store. If the product is of high value or mass product, then this will be attractive to any affiliate. However, affiliate marketing will be more suitable for selling digital (information) products with higher levels of commission, say ranging from 50 % to 75% per sale.

Coupons

Every shopping engine has a dedicated section to run promotions, set special offers like "free shipping" or "coupons".

Many web store owners forget to take advantage of these features and thereby enhance your visibility. Most shopping cart offers this feature on their templates.

Coupon promotion sites are excellent venues to promote your business and get more sales from these sources. Remember that coupon promotions should not be a routine feature, but use it judiciously so that it serves the purpose it intended for.

Pay per Click Advertising (PPC)/Cost per Click (CPC)

As the name indicates, PPC/CPC should be part of your marketing efforts to bring in the much-needed traffic (targeted traffic) to your web store.

Press releases, social media marketing etc can bring in good amount of traffic, but PPC can bring real buying customers to your site. However, you have to be very careful with PPC, because, it can cost you a fortune, if not used property.

As its name indicates, pay per click (PPC) advertising is that you place your ad in Google, Yahoo, Bing, Facebook, Amazon, or YouTube, when a customer clicks your ad; you pay a prefixed amount per click. The top most players in the PPC world are Google (Adwords and Admobi), Yahoo Search Marketing, Bing (MSN) - Ad Center, Facebook Ads, Amazon Ads, eBay Ads, Linked In ads, and Twitter Ads. Out of this, Google is the costliest and Facebook is the cheapest.

Google is the largest and topmost search engine in the world with about 77 percent share of the total online search volume followed by Bing and Yahoo. Hence, Google is a compulsory channel for your PPC advertising campaigns, because of the sheer volume of traffic it generates. However, Facebook with over 2061 million active user accounts is a dirt-cheap marketing channel for getting targeted traffic.

The ad programs from Facebook, Twitter, ezines and article directories (must be related to your niche), are most cost effective, less competition, targeted and therefore, can get more buying customers. However, you need to monitor and analyze the performance of these paid ads and concentrate on the most profitable programs.

YouTube

YouTube is the second largest search engine in the world. With over 1500 million active users, it is the largest video marketing channel in the world. According to a recent Nielsen survey, about 22 percent people watch video on internet and an astonishing 206 percent watch video on their mobile devises. YouTube has a daily view of over 400 million and an average 800 million views every month. Another survey conducted by Gallin group, it's found that 60 percent searchers reach YouTube, especially in the age group 18 –34 and an average time spent on YouTube is 167 minutes a month. Therefore, you must have a promotion portfolio in YouTube video marketing channel.

This again is an important low cost promotional channel for your business for getting targeted traffic to your site. YouTube is a free online video sharing channel.

You can upload your product video in YouTube and go viral. YouTube offers several features like, star rating, leave comment, and it shows the total number of views of the particular video.

How to Use YouTube for Business Growth

There are four steps involved in promoting your business through YouTube, viz. make a plan for how to create a strategy for your video, shooting your video, edit your videos with transitions, music and text overlays, and finally upload and publish your video to YouTube.

YouTube has created a separate eBook named "Play Book for Good" for the benefit of business owners for promoting business through YouTube. The eBook guides you through the entire process of creating a video, starting from planning, scripting, shooting, editing, uploading, and publishing your video. It also guides you through the process of promoting your videos viz, creating a channel, linking your website, updating your logo, building a community, and how to promote your business using various methods like social networking, offline, and advertising. You can down load this free pdf from YouTube web site.

Important Tip

Once you have finished adding tags, given description about your business or product that you want to promote, don't forget to give a unique channel name URL (give one of your top keyword on the channel URL name box,
e.g. http://www.youtube.com/channel/yourbusiness or product name.

Email Marketing

Even before starting your web store, you must start collecting leads. Otherwise, how do you get sales? How do you do that?

My dear friend, it is just simple. Get the help of a reputed email marketer, who will help you to set up an email capture opt-in page and through polls, surveys or just by creating a sample web page based on your topic or product, can be promoted through PPC.

This way you will be able to know where you stand and adjust according to the outcome of the initial survey, poll, or PPC campaign so that you do not waste valuable resources and most importantly, money. Email marketing and Direct Mail or Text messaging (this is for the Mobile devise) must have an important place in your marketing efforts to get more customer s, in particular repeat business from the same customers.

How do you do it?

Email marketing must always be permission based, whether it is internet or mobile based. This can be done through an opt-in or subscription page on your web site. However, it will be better to direct the visitor to a landing page specifically created for this purpose.

Landing Page

As the name indicates, the landing page is a special page created on your web site to receive the visitor to collect her personal information like name, email address and other information. It is where your visitors land after clicking a call-to-action on your website, blog, offer, or pay-per-click ad on social networks. On your landing page, your visitors will find a form that they can fill out to receive their offer.

How to entice the visitor to part with personal information?

Offer the visitor with a free offer of something, like a special e-book about the benefit of using your product, a how to video, a catalog, or a discount coupon, which can be used for a purchase or can be shared with friends and relatives.

Research has shown that by keeping relevant, focused and important information on a single page can increase conversion by 55 percent. Therefore, please ensure that the landing page has the following elements incorporated on it to ensure that the landing page is flawless.

A compelling Headline

With an average online attention span of 8 seconds, it is important that your headline sum up the offer as clearly and concisely as possible.

Content and Copy

Effective landing page copy provides more than just a plain description of what the offer is. It also gives visitors an incentive to download by conveying the value of the offer. You will wish to highlight the benefits of your offer with a brief paragraph or a few bullet points.

Your copy should emphasize how the offer addresses a specific problem, need, or interest your target audience cares about.

The Image

Research has shown that about 90 percent of information transmitted to the brain is visual and visuals are processed 60000 times faster in the brain than text. Therefore, incorporating images is an effective way to entice visitors and convey the purpose of your landing page, and why, they should download your offer. The images should be captivating and relevant to your offer.

The Layout

Primarily, the landing page layout should be simple. Determine what you want your visitors to do and create a layout that directs them through the steps. Convey the top three or four most important pieces of information almost immediately.

Use bullet points, numbering, and bold or italicized text to simplify the visual layout and highlight the focus points.

Create a page format that is as easy as possible for visitors to understand the offer, the value, and the action they need to take.

Navigation

To reduce the likelihood of your page, visitors clicking away, and roaming other parts of your website, remove all navigation and links from the page. By doing this, you will be eliminating any distractions from completing your form. By avoiding top navigation and links will help conversion rates on your landing pages.

Meta Descriptions and Keywords

Your Meta description will tell visitor s about the content on your landing page. These embedded descriptions are usually pulled by search engines, and shows in the search results. Meta descriptions are limited to 150 characters, therefore, ensure to make them short and clear explanations of your offer. The Meta data and keywords are both factors in how Google's ranking algorithm determines the relevance of your ads and where your website shows up in search results.

Another reason is because the description is the text that is shown and shared in social media. Also make sure that the text to be concise and convincing enough to attract visitors to your landing page.

The Form

The form is the main purpose of your landing page, as your ultimate goal is to get your visitors to fill it out.

Focus on the design and formatting of your landing page, because they have a direct impact on your conversion rates. Your form should appear above the fold and remove the need for visitors to scroll-down. Immediate visibility is important to draw the viewer's attention to the form.

Further, in order to get quality leads, use longer forms with required fields to collect enough data, but don't ask for too much information especially information that won't help you qualify your lead. Sometimes, people may be hesitant to provide sensitive information, especially online. In order to reassure your visitor, provide a link to your privacy policy p age.

You can also use client testimonials, authority endorsements, third-party security certifications, or guarantee seals. The credibility of your site and it looks will influence conversion rates.

Call-to-Action Buttons

In most forms, you will notice that the default text is "Submit", but data shows that landing pages with buttons labeled "Register Now" or Download Now" has more conversion. Try to make your buttons engaging and relevant to your offer. Experiment with different wording and focus on using language that will make visitors want to click the button instead of language that will scare them away.

Share the Links

The final aspect of a good landing page is to provide a link to social media networks on the landing page so that your visitors can be encouraged to share and forward your contents and offers, to their friends, friends of friends and peer groups, and they can be requested to promote your offer. By sharing your information or offer, you get more visitors and more visitors' means more lead, which can result is more revenue for you.

Business Blog

Blogs are the most preferred information channel for news feeds, search engines and even marketers. You must have a business blog (not personal blog) incorporated on your web site so that more information about your products and services can be provided to prospective buyers.

You can use business blogs for getting subscription to your newsletters, promoting campaigns and discount coupons. Your shopping cart must have the blog feature incorporated on it. If it is not there, please do not forget to get it.

How to Create Content for your Business Blog?

Unlike personal blogs, a business blog needs to provide more focused and most relevant content since a visitor takes hardly 3 seconds to gather information about your topic. Therefore, the following aspects will give you more advantage.

The first thing you should do is to identify a detailed picture of your target audience in order to create optimal content for them.

Who are your ideal customers and prospects? What are their biggest concerns, needs, and interests? Where can you find them – on search engines, social – media, or blogs and what kinds of content do they prefer?

These questions will help you develop buyer profiles. Marketing studies have shown that certain types of content play important roles at specific stages of the decision-making process. Here is a suggested mapping of buying stage to content type.

Create awareness, using blog posts, and social networks, through one-to-one interaction. After gathering information from various sources, the prospective customers do research for potential solutions. Here you can provide various types of resources like an e-book, webinars, or industry or niche related materials to generate more inter est in your products or services.

The next stage is the process of comparison. The prospect examines various options and narrows the list of sellers. This is the ideal time to offer the prospect case studies, demos, or testimonials i.e. social proof for inducing her to buy your product.

Finally, the prospect takes the decision to buy from whom. This stage is very crucial. At this stage, please provide her with latest analytical reports or detailed product information, especially, benefits of using your product to enable her to take the final decision.

Mobile Marketing

With the advent of modern communication devises like mobile phones, smartphones, tablets and retina devises, the way communication is done has changed a lot. Smartphone and tablets usage has been increasing rapidly and has overtaken the traditional Desktops and laptops.

As of 2016, there are over 6 billion mobile users worldwide and this figure is expected to be around 7.7

billion by the year 2020. According to the latest mobile usage statistics, there are over 1.2 billion people, accessing internets from their mobile devises, viz. smartphones, and Tablets. In US alone 265 m and expected to be 276 m by 2020.

In the US 87%, adults own a mobile, 60% people use their smartphones while in the shop and 95% smartphone owners search for local information. 44% Americans sleep with their mobiles nearby, because they don't want to miss a notification. Therefore, If you are a local business owner or would be owner of a brick and mortar business, then you cannot be ignorant about the advantages of using Mobile Marketing and in particular Text Messaging and Multimedia Marketing for growing your business and increasing the Return on Investment (RoI).

Text Messaging

SMS is passé. It is text-messaging time now. The growth of mobile population has thrown open the avenues for marketers with text messaging to geo target customers and increase business growth and customer retention.

According to Mobile marketer survey, 64% smartphone users have made a purchase after seeing a mobile ad. However, 74% did not receive any mobile ads from their favorite brands. That means, a large number of local businesses can increase brand awareness and increase business growth through mobile marketing using a mix of permission-based text messaging, multimedia marketing and mobile advertising.

In order to be successful, particularly, local businesses like food and beverages, travel, entertainment, tourism, retail, have to target local customers and prospects using a combination of mobile advertising and social media advertising using PPC/CPC. The best options are through Google's Admob, Facebook Ad, Twitter (Promoted) Tweets, LinkedIn ad, and YouTube promotions using multimedia content.

Mobile Audio Advertising

If you are in the business of music streaming, applications and games, don't forget to provision for mobile audio advertising as it is catching up fast and can captivate a specific targeted audience, who are willing to listen, socially connected and responsive to audio advertising.

Audio advertising is more responsive than video or display as mood-based advertising is more relevant and engaging, which can increase one-to-one engagement. For any marketer, the importance of using mobile as a media of marketing cannot be ignored.

Online Advertising giant Google has captured a market share of 95% of search based mobile advertising segment, which is growing at a fast pace. If you are not familiar with mobile marketing, please do a local internet search and you will be able to find many mobile marketing and text messaging service providers in your area. However, for your convenience, I have given a few names of the most popular service providers in the chapter dealing with Essential Tools and Service.

Mobile marketing, using text messaging in combination with multimedia and social networks, is very cost effective and result oriented. However, mobile advertising to be more successful, a reward based approach can get more positive responses since every one like to get something in return, may be a coupon, an e- book, a free ticket and so on.

New technologies like Quick Response or Quick Reader (QR) codes and Near Field Communication (NFC) enable people to interact with each other and gather information or compare product features, price etc. and will be able to make purchase decisions fast.

Quick Response (QR) Codes

What is a QR code? Quick Response (QR) codes are used to take a piece of information from a transitory media and put it in to your cell phone or smartphone. Most smartphones are scanner enabled to read QR codes. QR codes will give you details about the business and allow users to search for nearby locations or show you a URL, or details of products, offers, contacts, events, competition, a coupon, social network IDs or a link to your YouTube video.

Using mobile apps and cloud based marketing tools, retailers/shop owners are able to manage content delivery and offers to shoppers, thereby enhance customer experience, and retain customer loyalty.

You will be surprised to know that permission based Text Messaging gets more positive results. Almost 98% open within 15 minutes of receiving a text message. However, please remember that don't overdo it. Ideally, once a month messaging is quite effective and can draw more customers to your doorstep.

Some of the most popular text messaging service providers are MoneyMailer, iLoopMobile, Foursquare, MobiQpons, CouponSherpa, and Yowza. All these Apps are very useful in establishing brands, and helping

105

agencies create effective mobile marketing campaigns though text message and mobile activity with customers.

In case these type of companies are not available in your area, do a web search and find out companies that provide service in your area, city, or country.

However, since Google's Admob is the undisputed market leader with over 95% of search based mobile marketing share, you must have a portfolio of advertising program (PPC) with their Admob.

Advantages of Mobile Marketing

Some important usages of mobile marketing are: Sponsorship of event activation. You can conduct live voting, deliver coupons and incentives, which is available always, and are quite effective. The recent innovations like the mobile wallet marketing e.g. Apple Passbook and Google Wallet are quite popular with customers.

Use Mobile marketing to keep your most valuable customers connected to your brand. You can include mobile as an extension of your existing loyalty program, rewarding customers with exclusive announcements and repeat purchase incentives. This way mobile extension can increase your customer base and profitability, all these, at a low cost.

Mobile Commerce [M-Commerce]

The phenomenal growth of mobile communication devises like cell phones, smartphones, and tablets has changed the way people do purchases. A large number of people use their smartphones for buying products online, in-store and on the move. This trend has created an opportunity for Mobile banking and Mobile commerce or M-Commerce, which is growing very fast.

All major online market places like eBay, Amazon and a host of other small, medium and large online retailers use Mobile commerce in their business. So, please don't forget to offer the mobile payment facility to your customers when selecting a payment gateway.

Local Listings

Local listing in Google Places, Yahoo Local, and similar other local online sources where you can list your web site for free and get good amount of free traffic to your site. Listing in these sites should be done on priority basis in the beginning itself as most shoppers search locally for products and services.

Forums

Forums are an excellent place to interact with prospective customers and experts to gather information and exchange views. In my opinion a business owner must spend at least an hour a week at appropriate forums related to your product/niche. You can decide when and where to spend your valuable time.

However, please ensure that you go to the forums, which are timely, relevant, and useful to your type of business. There are all types of forums, which ar e not at all useful and a time waste, especially those business forums discussing about MLM, Ad networks, paid surveys, black hat methods and so on. Please avoid these types of forums.
There are large numbers of forums related to small business or home based and micro business. Some of them are government sponsored, some are professional

bodies, and some run by expert individuals. Websites/organizations like sba.gov (US small business Administration), open forum.com (promoted by American Express Group), all business. foxbusiness.com, startupnation.com from VeriSign, cosboa.org.au.

The Council of small Business Australia, fsb.org, UK, and becaustralia.org are some good places you can hang around.

Yellow Pages

You may not get many sales through this media. However, one advantage of using Yellow pages is that you may get a back link from some sites, and perhaps you can get more visibility through listing in the local yellow pages, especially, Craigslist and Yellow Pages in the US, or similar one in your location.

In India, Just Dial and India Mart are good ones. There are many other business directories both B2B and B2C are there.

Article Marketing

Article marketing is another most important channel for promoting your web store. You write articles about your store and products and submit them to popular article directories, and blog sites relevant to your niche. You can also publish articles along with product details in Web 2 properties.

A small Tip

In order to get a back link as well as more targeted visitors to your site, please write content in the 400-500 words range and not to include most important keywords in it.

Instead, use a related keyword, in the article title and contents using different variations of the keyword, so that the main contents with most relevant keywords will be available only on your web site or blog and not elsewhere.

However, this channel is mostly used by blog writers for promoting others web sites for getting targeted visitors, who will clicking the ads on their site and a small commission.

User Generated Content

What is user generated content? It is nothing but as the name indicates, content contributed by your own followers or visitors to the site. In the past, sites like Facebook, Twitter, YouTube, Pinterest etc. they all grown to gigantic sizes, not because it has generated and placed all the information there. It is public generated content viz. videos, news, pictures, and all that helped them to grow. Therefore, if you want to grow your site, use this popular technique to grow your brand or business. You can even reward the best content contributors.

There is growing evidence to show that more are more brands and marketers are using user generated content to grow their traffic and increased interaction with visitors.

Some of the platforms you can use for user-generated content on your sites are Ning, Socialgo, and Grou.ps etc. You can even provide a space on your web site or blog for users to contribute contents relevant to your niche/product/service.

Classified Ads

Use eBay's free classified ads like ebayclassified.com, and paid classifieds from eBay.com or other similar shopping and comparison sites to take advantage of their huge targeted traffic to your site.

Offline Promotions

As the adage goes, you should not restrain yourself to a few channels of promotion. In addition to online channels, you should also try off line channels especially local ones, like newspaper advertisement, specialized magazines, local yellow pages, radio, and television, local trade promotion agencies like Chamber of Commerce to take advantage of their huge popularity. Through referral programs and direct contact with your existing customers, you can achieve about 40 to 50 percent increase in sales.

Seminars and exhibitions will also be very beneficial. Using your customer database, initiate email marketing (permission based) with free newsletters, product catalogs, offers and coupons. This type of promotions will be most cost effective and gets positive results.

Use of Social Media for Marketing

Most businesses across the world increasingly use social media for interacting with prospects and customers to gain more and more foot hold in the market, gaining brand image and recommendations.

Social media like Facebook, Google Plus, Twitter, Linkedin, YouTube, Pinterest, all has become so popular with people. Therefore, no one can ignore the importance of social media as a marketing tool.

However, caution must be taken that you are not taken for a ride by unscrupulous social media paid promotion offers of getting you so many likes, followers and so on. Instead, use the paid promotion programs of reputed social networks directly.

How to Use Facebook

Some of the important features of Facebook for business are: News feed, Promoted post, and FBXchange. The major benefits of a promoted post is that it increases the likelihood of seeing your post, see your message in their news feeds, become aware of your business and respond to a discount or sales promotion.

Facebook has provided detailed information and guidance about promoting your business using various features. You can down load it from Facebook's web site.

How to use Twitter for Marketing

In Twitter's own words, the guidelines they provide for creation of a profile or business page is as follows. Since it is the entry point, incorporate your brand name in the Twitter profile.

You can include photos, bio and links. Use creative elements like a custom background or header image to give a better look to your profile. Select the best username, which is your Twitter URL. Eg (write your brand or store name here). Once @yourbusiness selected the perfect username, don't forget to include it in all your marketing materials viz. web site, letter head, visiting card and publicity materials so that your customers and partners know where to find you.

The next step will be to introduce you. Write a shorter, clear, concise bio that describes your brand, products or services. Do not forget to include a trackable link to your main website or to a specific landing page to drive traffic to your site.

Twitter has provided detailed information and guidance about promoting your business using various features of Twitter. You can down load it from Twitter's web site. Use of Hash Tag in Promoting your Business What is a hash tag? The hash # symbol is extensively used in promoting a business or brand through social networking, and especially Twitter to indicate a prominent keyword or phrase in your tweets. For example #love is the most popular hash tag.

The #hash tag was first used in Twitter tweets. Hash tag is used for promoting a brand, business or indicating trends. Now, it is being used extensively in most social networks like Facebook, Google+, Pinterest, and so on. When used properly, you get better results in search results and more page views and followers through social networking sites.

YouTube

Do your Research

Before creating and uploading your video in You Tube, don't forget to do your research to find out what type of keywords are used in optimizing similar videos in You Tube, related to your product/niche. This will help you find out what keywords are popular and what types of videos get maxi mum views. The popularity of a video can be assessed by the views count. It is important to note that there are two ways that video sults are returned (i) "the title" of the video and (ii) 'tags'.

The 'tags' used to describe the video are the most important keyword reference to optimize your web pages. With over 1500 million active user base, it is one of the best marketing promotion media for any enterprise.

Sort Your Search Results

Search results can be sorted by date added, view count, rating, or relevance to keyword. The main sort feature you will want to use is view count because this will show you which videos are getting the maximum views.

Success Tips

Use the search refinement features when doing keyword research. After creating a YouTube account and uploaded some videos, take the time to create a custom profile and your own custom channel information. You should also create at least one group, and you may want to create a playlist if you have more than one video. This will give you a big advantage when people search for ' Channels', 'Groups', and 'Playlists'.

Research is the key to success. It is impossible to do all the work manually; hence, special tool for finding stealth keywords and optimizing web page/videos using SEO.

What will make your video successful?

Here is the list: Funny, Weird, Gross (fear factor), Shocking, Interesting, Sexy, Inspiring, Demonstrates, Instructional and Personal. These 10 factors influence the success of a video.

Important Facts about Success of YouTube Videos Number of views is not a criterion for assessing the success of a video. People get bored if the length of the video is too large.   The ideal length is about 1 to 2 minutes, because people do not have that, much attention spans.

Product demo videos get more targeted visitors. Demonstrations of a product using YouTube can help to sell a product. A demonstrational video that does not get many views from people searching YouTube, it can still be a useful marketing device - just embed the demonstrational video in your website to help convert visitors into buyers. It is a good idea to put people in the video so that it goes viral many times.

The point about branding your video with video editing software is that you want to be subtle enough with your branding that your video does not look only like an ad. Yet you do not want to be so subtle that people, who like your video and like what you are all about, cannot easily find more information.

The style of branding you use depends on what you want to accomplish as well as your personal preferences. Windows moviemaker is good free video editing software, which you can use to create videos.

Uploading videos

You can save your videos in the following formats .mpeg, .mov, .avi, .wmv and flash videos in .flv format and then upload it.

Specific Tactics for Marketing

Building a Community on YouTube:
Create a YouTube Group for getting subscribers to your YouTube videos.

Promoting Your Own Products with YouTube

Create an eBook Trailer demonstrating your product.
Promoting Business Opportunities Market Yourself.

List Building

Build your List by Offering Free Videos

Use video to build a Personal Relationship with your subscribers.

Educational Sample Videos.
Use video testimonials by customers using your product.

YouTube videos as content for your site.
Embed videos demonstrating your product, to keep visitors at your own site.
Make your videos go viral

Post a YouTube video to your Facebook, Twitter, Linkedin or to a Blog. Also, mail video URLs to friends and family, informing media outlets offering your Video as content to other popular websites in your Niche.
Radio Advertising

One of the most popular and instant response media is radio advertising.   Whether it is for brand building or quick response.

First, it is cheap compared to other media like newspaper, TV channels, even social media advertising.   Here the response is specific and quick, because you get the immediate attention of the customer as he/she in front of the voice.

Second, it can be used anywhere, be it be at home, while doing any work, or travelling, listeners can hear the sound and the matter advertised very clearly and quickly.

There are certain specific requirements while doing the marketing campaign.

First of all, you must clearly specify the purpose of your advertisement through radio, whether it is for mass brand building or for capturing a specific target group.

Next, you must be very clear about your target customer, i.e. demographic specific, whether it is a home maker, a teenager, a music fan, you can split the groups in to very specific target audience viz. a rock music fan, a dance enthusiast, a coffee lover, etc. The details can be worked out with your radio advertiser and finalize the ad format.

To get a good response from target audience, the ad needs to be repeated at least three times at different intervals and that too immediately before or after a popular program and not along with cluttered ads.
You must add a popular human voice or some kind of specific tunes, voices of animals, birds, or babies crying, laughing, or such things to get quick recollection.

The ideal time to advertise for a target group is when the customer is on the way to shopping. This method is proven and gets good response as the information is in her head all the time while on the way to shopping place.

However, for each need and target group you have to identify the ideal time for each group and the radio advertiser can provide you this information.

Audience Polls

It will be a good idea to conduct an audience poll through discussion forums. Alternatively through other channels like Facebook, Linkedin, About.com or Google/ Yahoo/ Bing PPC ads and collecting responses through an opt in page with the help of a good email marketing service provider. This will give you deep insights into what is the look and feel of your audience and market, what product or service they are interested.

Chapter 9

ESSENTIAL TOOLS
AND SERVICES

This step includes the essential tools and services; how to use them, where to get it, and related information.

The Business Planner

PaloAlto.com

Most individuals who ventures into starting a new business may not have any idea about how to make a business plan. It is very important to know the basic aspects of your proposed business before you spend any money on your business, which includes infrastructure, stock, or services.

The idea of a business plan is to know where you stand. If you know beforehand the destination, it is very easy for you to reach there without any difficulty. Similarly, in the beginning, if you know what exactly needed to start and grow a business, your journey, as a business owner will be more comfortable.

You can see sample business plans related to several categories of businesses at PaloAlto.com You may alter the plans to suit your requirements by adding or deleting certain items so that it reflects your business plan as a whole, and in particular, gives an idea where you stand and can take corrective measures, if necessary.

In case you wish to avail financing from banks or other lending institutions, you need a highly professional looking Business Plan. PaloAlto Software group is the creators of the most popular Business Plan Pro, Sales and Marketing Pro, and Live Plan software.

All these products are highly professional and most popular. Therefore, you get all the tools to create an impressive business plan or a sales and marketing plan. With the above products, you can create business plans for your own use, or use the software for creating highly professional business and sales plans and sell that as a service to prospective customers for a good profit.

Alternately, you have to approach a chartered accountant for getting a business plan, which normally are not a cheap proposition.

Market Place/Sales Platform

Amazon.com

Amazon is the most trusted an d the world's largest online store, especially for physical products, with an integrated operation across the globe. They also provide training, tutorials, and tools for selling products online on listing basis or through their Amazon Web Store for promoting your products with your own domain name and Amazon cloud hosting. Amazon provides everything you need to run your business in a few hours, including payment gateway.

eBay.com

eBay is the largest online auction site with operations in Europe, United States, Australia and Asia including India. You sell items on auction basis or on fixed price basis. eBay provides you all the tools and services you need to run you business, including payment gateway.

They charge a listing fee and transaction fee based on selling price. They offer all the required training and tutorials for your success. Get more information from the eBay web site.

Payment Gateway

Once you have decided about the market place/platform or popularly known as the Shopping Cart to sell your products or service separately as an independent vendor, then you need a mechanism to collect the payments from customers. There are several well know payment gateway service providers of international repute. However, selecting the best service provider is a gigantic task.

Each one claims to be the best and boast of charging you the least fees. However, it is not that easy to get all information. If someone charges less transaction fee, there may be some kind of hidden fees like monthly service fees related to your account, statement fee etc.

In some other cases, payment gateway providers charge several fees like set up fee, monthly processing fee and an each transaction fee. Therefore, in order to make you comfortable, I have done the research for you and listed here the best, most reliable, fees are at comfortable level, and very transparent about all charges. You may select any one from the service provider listed below, which you feel suits your requirement.

Amazon Secure Pay

Amazon secure pay is from the house of Amazon, the reputed online ecommerce platform trusted by millions all over the world. The best thing about Amazon payment is that you do not have to pay any set up fee, monthly fee, cancellation fee, or fraud protection fees.

The charges include everything in it. Moreover, you get peace of mind. Their current fee starts at 2.9% + $0.30 for transaction of $10 or more and there are various slabs and the higher the volume of sale, lower the fees, which comes down to 1.9% + $0.30. There may be some changes in the fees, which you may verify with Amazon.

Paypal.com

PayPal is one of the most popular alternative payment gateways, owned by eBay. They provide all kinds of transaction facilitation service for physical, digital and subscription products. Their transaction fees are very reasonable and no set up fee or monthly payment commitment.

PayPal's current transaction fees ranges between 2.9% +$0.30 and 4.4% + $0.30, for each transaction, depending upon volume of business. There may be some changes in the fees, which you may verify with PayPal.

Authorizenet.com

Authorize net is owned by Cyber Source Corporation, a wholly owned subsidiary of VISA, for payment processing. The current fees charged by Authorizenet.com is as follows. Set up fee $99.00 (one time pay), Monthly gateway fee - $20.00/ month, Transaction fee $0.10 for each transaction, and batch fee $0.25 for each batch. They provide payment processing for credit card, online and digital download payments. There may be some changes in the fees, which you may verify with Authorizenet.

CCAvenue.com

CC Avenue is an India based payment gateway provider and is one of the best and cheapest, in terms of transaction fee, set up fee and other fees. They operate in South Asian markets. They have three types of packages viz. Free, Premium, and Privilege.

Google Wallet

Google wallet offers a variety of programs in partnership with business partners and a host of other loyalty program providers. Google's transaction fees are very reasonable and ranges between 1.9% + $0.30 and 2.9% + $0.30 for different slabs. There are no other fees. However right now, their services are available only in the US.

Rupay

Rupay is a new payment gateway from National Payment Corporation of India, similar to Visa and MasterCard, developed specifically for the Indian customers. Their fees are very small and most reliable, secure and trustworthy. You can get the details from their web site http://www.npci.org.in

After simplification of doing business in India, there are a few more excellent payment facilitators in India, that includes, wallets from all most all nationalized and private banks and private player, especially PAYTM is one of the most popular and leading wallets in India.

Amazon and eBay profitability analysis

ShowMyProfits.com (suitable only for US business)

Show my profits are a pc based software very useful for online business owners who are selling on Amazon and eBay. This tool will provide you instant information about the profitability of your product that you are planning to sell on the above sites. This is an essential tool for online sellers.

Terapeak.com

Terapeak is the leader in ecommerce market analytics, dedicated to helping online merchants to grow their business and become more profitable. Terapeak software solution provides market data analysis for eBay, and Amazon. It provides sales, marketing, and other input (ecommerce) data (of previous months/year, category wise) for business analysis.

The data is very valuable and essential for making business decisions and product promotion as well as to generate more revenue and profits with lesser efforts and more intelligence. More details are available at their web site.

Hammertap.com

It is another business analytical data provider similar to Terapeak. Hammertap's philosophy is to follow the dictum - Research, Source, and Sell. It advises its member subscribers to source products based on research data and intelligence and list your products and price right to earn the best margins and profits.

Hammertap suggests you to source products through drop shipping to test market and then include Light Bulk Wholesalers to increase profits. Then start importing to further increase your earnings and finally include Liquidations to offer loss leader s and limited-time offers. The difference between Hammertap and Terapeak is only in the fee structure. Since both Terapeak and Hammertap get data from the same source, you get excellent tips and advices on how to research and list your products in eBay and Amazon for greater profits.

Multi Channel Ecommerce

If you are an experienced online seller and wants to spread your business to multiple channels, then you must think about opting for multi channel ecommerce software service. I have found two great services, the US based Vendio and UK based SellerExpress.

Vendio.com

Vendio (owned by Alibaba.com) provides the leading multi-channel ecommerce software platform for small and mid-sized online businesses. Vendio simplifies the process of selling across multiple online channels like eBay, Amazon, Facebook and your own store, by providing a centralized inventory management system, order processing and tracking, customer communication, marketing tools, and other productivity-enhancing applications.

Vendio provides a fully customizable online store with integrated shopping cart to every merchant for no additional cost, all through one integrated, cloud-based interface.

Sellerexpress.com

SellerExpress multi channel ecommerce software is a complete package for managing every step of the — marketplace sales cycle inventory, auto price checking, order fulfillment, customer emails, shipping, currency conversion and much more. SellerExpress multi-channel ecommerce software service is for businesses to increase sales across Amazon, eBay, Play.com and own web store. It is a complete all-in-one inventory, order, and listings management software with a built-in auto re-pricer.

Optional Shopping Carts

I have done a thorough analysis of all the available shopping cart vendors and found that Shopping Cart Elite is the best amongst all shopping carts. However, those who cannot afford to buy their services, then Magentogo, and Shopify are the next best shopping carts available across the market in terms of benefits, features, and cost.

Shoppingcartelite.com

Shopping Cart Elite is an all-in-one, complete suite of ecommerce products made for the discerning online store owner, who is looking for every tool that he/she requires, is provided at one place. No fear of failure of add-ons, technical jargons etc.

In addition, many optional plug-in are also available on additional payments on monthly basis. In case you are unable to bear the cost of Shopping Cart Elite, then only, I suggest other rated carts like Magentogo or Shopify.

Magentogo.com

Magentogo (owned by eBay Inc.) is a very advanced shopping cart for well-experienced small businesses. It offers advanced features and many add-ons to enhance user experience. Magentogo's features include Marketing, promotion, and conversion tools, site management, Search Engine Optimization, catalog management, product browsing, checkout, payment and shipping, order management, customer care, customer account, international support, mobile commerce, Analytics and Reporting.

Shopify.com

Shopify is another good ecommerce shopping cart especially for small businesses, with all the features you need for running an online store. They offer free and paid templates including many premium and exclusive themes, which can be customized. Without any hassle, you can set up your store in a few hours and start accepting orders. Their CMS (Content Management System) is very simple.

It comes with a built-in blogging platform, which is necessary for any business to provide information to prospects and customers, do many things like promoting coupons, conducting surveys and customer comments.
It also comes with many apps for enhanced features for your web store.

Keyword Research Tool

Market Samurai.com

This is an essential and must have tool for keyword research, product/niche selection, competition, profitability and commerciality analysis, link building, and monetization tools including article generation and promotion especially in the early stages of your business. It does all the manual work, which can take all your time, in minutes, efficiently, and neatly.

Use Market Samurai in combination with Google Planner (Keyword Tool) and Google Trends, a free tool from

Google can make wonders to your business. This is a software tool for which you have to pay only once and the price is very low.

Note

However, please note that this tool is only for the micro or small niches and not useful for any other small medium or large business. For them Google Planner along with any of the following services will be the best option. Alternately you can outsource the services from different agencies that provide this type of services.

SpyFu.com

This is an optional, but essential tool at an advanced stage of your business. SpyFu exposes the search marketing secret formula of your most successful competitors. It searches for any domain and see every place they have shown up on Google: every keyword they have bought on Adwords, every organic rank, and every ad variation in the last 6 years. Learn how to connect these domains, too.

SpyFu is a hosted software service for doing keyword research, ppc and competition analysis. At some point of time, especially when you learnt all aspects of online marketing and wish to branch out to new areas and product lines, then you need the services of a software service like Spyfu, for getting more market and competition information.

Ubersuggest.com:

A very good tool for expanded keyword ideas and the beauty is that it is free. They get the feed from Google API and hence the lists of keywords are worth its weight.

Search Engine Optimization (SEO)

Webceo.com

Webceo is one of the leading search engine optimization software service providers. They have an online version as well as a desktop version for SEO. They offer three variants of the online software viz. for individuals, for teams, and B2B. The online version of the software includes the following individual components i.e. Keyword Tool, Rank Checker, Website SEO Auditor, Web analytics, Content Submission, Social Buzz tracker and SEO Checklists.

iBusinessPromoter.com

Another great SEO software provider is IBP. This software works on a PC and can be used for SEO, link building, directory submission, competition analysis, content submission, rank checking, and comes with a top ten guarantee in Google search results in a one-year period, for the select keywords that you choose.

Apps for Mobile

The Growing number of mobile users necessitates you to go in for APPs (short for application, a software), which can be downloaded into any mobile devices or a PC. This will enable users to download information, whether product or service related, even a web page can be down loaded using an app, into mobile devises like smartphones and tablets.

Here is a list of most popular and best in class, both free and paid apps creating software/service providers.

Free
1. Yapp.us
2. Appgeyser.com
3. Appsbar.com
4. Shortstack.com - free up to 2000 fans. Exceeding that, paid service only.

Paid

Appypie.com

Appypie is a cloud based DIY (do it yourself) Mobile App Builder or App Creation Software. This is a simple but hybrid platform to build Apps without any programming or coding skills and can be built for Android, iPhone, iPad, Windows Phone and Blackberry and publish to Google Play and iTunes.

Tabsite.com

This is one of the best in class ready-made social engagement app service provider. The various types of apps include web site re-sizer, contests, and sweepstakes for various networks like Facebook, Twitter , Pinterest, Instagram, Linkedin, YouTube, and a host of other networks. Adding Bells and Whistles to your Web Store.

Special tool for enhancing Image Quality

Magictoolbox.com

Magic Toolbox is a web master's special tool for making the web a more beautiful and engaging place and web store owners' must have feature, if affordable. Magic Zoom i mage tools give anybody with 5 minutes, the power to create gorgeous effects on their websites, with zoom, enlarge, 360° and slideshow features. Each tool enables web designer s to create amazing user experiences with their high- resolution images, leading to better conversion, higher sales, and lower returns.

Selling Information Products

When it comes to selling information (digital) products online, there are a few very popular places where you can sell your eBooks, DVD, CD, pdf, music or even software. That too without paying any membership fee, admission fee or such fees at all. You may come several paid listing places, but my personal advice is to keep away from such paid services. Why should you pay a fee for listing your items, when you can get better quality, well- reputed places, free of cost?

However, all the companies that promote your e-products will charge a fee for doing the distribution and selling. That is genuine and acceptable. Normally most distributors take a fee of about 20 to 30 per cent and in some cases up to 50 per cent of the sale value. The industry average is 20 per cent.

Kindle Direct Publishing (by Amazon)

You can sell information products (eBooks) through their network of sites across many countries and they have a lending service through Amazon Prime, known as KDP Select.

However, to participate in the lending program, you have to give exclusive right of distribution to Amazon, but according to me it is a very good program as Amazon controls about 65% of the eBook market. However, some of you may not like to give exclusive right of distribution to Amazon. No problem, you can opt for specific markets.

Createspace.com (owned by Amazon)

At Createspace, you can publish and sell real books both paper back and hard bound. They also distribute your Books, DVD, CD, not only to Amazon; it will distribute to most reputed online booksellers thorough its network. They also provide an extended distribution service.

They will provide the tools you require to convert your products into different formats including the eBook/book cover design software. In addition, they have professionals to do all your works like, editing, review and design of the pages and cover.

Smashwords.com

Another most reputed information product distributor is Smashwords. Smashwords distributes to all the reputed online product distribution channels. The beauty with this company is that they provide all the information you required to promote you and your products. All their services are free. They also have paid professional services like, editing, review, and formatting of your products by experts, including cover creation.

Barnesandnoble.com

The world's second largest distributors of eBooks, eReader (Nook), Books, CDs, DVDs, Magazines and a host of other items.

Kobo.com (a Rakuten company)

Kobo is the third largest online eBook distributors in the world. Their eReaders are quite popular.

Lulu.com

Lulu is another important information product (digital products), distribution company of repute. They also publish books on demand and distribute your products internationally through their distribution channel. Like other most reputed digital products distributors, Lulu also offer professional services like editing, cover design, digital conversion etc., of cour se, for a fee.

Google Play, iTunes (owned by Apple), instagram are other important places you can sell your information products, especially Mobile Apps.

Other Useful Sites

Ganxy.com, Gumroad.com and Instamojo.com are the places where you can sell digital products independently, through their market place and all the three charges a flat fee of about 5 to 5.5% including the PayPal payment gateway fee. These places are ideal for selling products at higher prices than the above major distribution channels.

Tools for eBook Authors

The main tool for an eBook author is the text conversion software and the plagiarism checker software. There are free as well as paid (both one time and recurring) software available in the market. However, only very few can boast they are good at what we want i.e. usefulness and reliability.

All the above listed eBook distribution service providers offer free tools for converting your digital products. For eBook conversion, under the free category, there are two software available free to down load from the internet. They are: Calibre and Sigil. Calibre is not a conversion software, but mostly a reading device conversion tool. It can convert the text into most e-reader formats viz. Kindle, Nook, .mobi, epub etc.

A Small Tip

In order to convert your .doc/.docx or .txt or .rtf or .pdf files, first save the file into a .html file by saving the file using your MS word. i.e. using the save as, other option and then selecting the web page filtered option to save it into a .htm or .html file. Then convert it into .mobi, epub, AZ3 (for KF8) or other formats using Calibre.

Since caliber is not a tool for authors, you need editing software. Sigil is a very good free tool for editing HTML files, which you can down load from internet.

Note: *Kindle Direct Publishing or KDP, provide free conversion tool namely, Kindle Publisher, which you can down load from their site and save it on your computer. Then convert your .doc or .docx i.e. word file into KDP format usable in all devises. Alternately, you can submit the word document direct in the uploading document page and it converts the word file into digital format. This is very simple and easy.*

Product Sourcing

As already explained in the main chapters, once you have decided about your niche/ product/ group of products, the next step is to identify suppliers for the product(s) that too, quality must be good, price should be reasonable, and above all the supplier must be reliable and trustworthy.

How do you know the supplier you selected is reliable and trustworthy? It is difficult to know this, but if there are some reliable agencies that are reputed, trustworthy and can be verified, then things will be easy for you.

I have done a thorough research and found out the most reliable wholesale supplier sources for you, so that you can concentrate on the main task i.e selling. My order of preference is as follows:

WorldWideBrands.com
Worldwide Brands, is a wholesale supplier source recommendation site promoted by Chris Malta and highly reputed, verifiable and carries the trust seal of BBB.

They operates in USA and UK markets and have about 8000 verified and tested wholesale suppliers and Drop shippers. They currently charge a onetime fee of $299 for their membership.

Salehoo.com

Another trustworthy and reliable source verified wholesale supplier source recommendation site. They have over 8000 verified legitimate wholesaler source. Salehoo carries the BBB trust logo. They charge an annual membership fee of $67. They provide complete training in addition to a niche of the month newsletter from their research lab.

Doba.com

Like worldwide brands and Salehoo, Doba is one of the largest and integrated drop shippers, especially for selling on eBay, and easily integrate with other shopping carts via API. Doba's Push to Marketplace, allows eBay drop shippers to select products from Doba's catalog and automatically push those products to live sales and auctions on eBay with just a few clicks of the mouse.

Doba is a membership based site and very good for beginners as well as experienced persons to sell products without investing in stocks. You can use the drop ship method i.e. you sell the products on eBay, collect payment and pay Doba and they in turn deliver the goods to the customer on your behalf.

Aliexpress.com

Every online seller wishes to have products sourced at lower rates and there is no other place than getting products from Asian countries, especially from China. However, there are many problems associated with products sourcing from China. They include fraud, quality, timely delivery, and above all communicating with Chinese suppliers. So what is the alternative?

When dealing with Chinese suppliers, wholesalers, or manufacturer s, you need to identify people who speak English well, have good reputation and feedback score and offer good quality and price. This will be a gigantic task for an ordinary mortal, but there are ways in which you can get your job done. They are: an Agent or Trading Company, a Customs broker and a Freight For warder.

However, it is not possible to deal with all three categories of people separately, but if you can get a three-in-one agency that did all your job viz. product sourcing, price negotiation, verification, customs clearance and freight forwarding/shipping. This is a difficult job but not impossible.

135

There are few good agencies that do all the three jobs for you and of all agencies the best one is Ali Express.com, part of Alibaba Group. Ali Express is in a position to source products for you, negotiate, and offer best price for you. The best thing about AliExpress is that you can get small quantities, a minimum of 3 pieces of any item and they offer free shipping for most items and on certain items, they add shipping cost to the total cost, separately.

Aliexpress offers a buyer protection. They keep your money in an escrow account and will be passed on to the supplier only after you satisfy and confirm the quality, quantity, and receipt of products. Until then, they keep the money in the escrow account and if you are not satisfied, the amount will be refunded to you.

Wholesalepages.co.uk

They source products exclusively for UK and European markets only. Their services are on membership basis. They have monthly, six monthly, yearly and lifetime membership fees.

TopTenWholesale.com

This US based B2B wholesale directory consisting of the top 10 US wholesalers, is one of the best source for wholesale buyers and suppliers. The JPC group consists of Top Ten Wholesale.com, Manufcturer.com, and WholesaleU.com, OffPriceNetwork.com, and Manufacturer.com, the Magazine. They offer a free membership as well as a premium membership.

Free Wholesale Sources

There are some reputed wholesale supplier sources; in fact, they are supplier directories, which is very useful for getting product information and find supplier sources.

Thewholesaleforums.co.uk

Wholesaleforums, UK is a free membership forum for you to find wholesalers, source products, stock, and access reviews of wholesale suppliers, get import/ export advice, essential business information, and support from over 100,000 members. The Wholesaleforums, UK is more suitable for Retailers, eBay sellers and Traders.

WholesaleCentral.com

Another excellent source for Wholesalers (B2B only) is the US based Sumner Communications Group (consisting of Fleamarketzone.com, Wholesale Central.com, and Closeout Cental.com). They also own the Independent Retailer.com. You may checkout these two sources, which are excellent place for product sourcing and product information.

Hktdc.com

The Hong Kong Trade Development Council (HKTDC) was established in 1966, and serves as a statutory body dedicated to promoting Hong Kong trade. Its mission is to create opportunities for Hong Kong companies, especially small and medium -sized enterprises, by promoting trade in goods and services globally. They have more than 40 overseas offices and 11 offices in Chinese mainland.

Most of their manufacturers and suppliers are verified by D&B (Doon and Bradstreet) and inspection done by Intertek a unit of Moody International. Very reliable and trustworthy. The only problem with them is the minimum order quantity is 100 pieces each, and in most cases, they have a minimum purchase amount in dollar terms.

Press Release, Marketing, and Promotion

PRWeb.Com

PRweb is currently the World's No.1 press release agency - the specialist who does the electronic promotion for you, which include, press release, announcement about your – organization a new product launch, current promotion, a local team sponsorship or whatever. There are various internationally reputed online PR agencies to do this job. They are the market leader and send your news to major search engines like Google, Yahoo, and Bing.

They distribute your press release to more than 30,000+ journalists and bloggers and opt-in news subscribers and host your news release on their web site, which receives over 3 million visitors each month, for future reference.

Benefits of using Press Releases

Create thousands of credible first impressions. Drive affordable and qualified traffic to your website. Generate publicity around your business and your products and help with search engine visibility. Complement your advertising, email marketing and pay-per-click efforts. Measure the immediate impact of your online marketing efforts through reporting tool.

OnlinePRMedia.com

Onlineprmedia is a specialized PR agency, providing services to small medium and large enterprises. They have various types of plans viz. social media press release, search engine visibility, and maximum visibility.

They also have a partnership with PRNewswire for specialized news releases.

eReleases.com

eReleases is another major press release agency, which also has a partnership with PRnewswire, the oldest PR firm in the corporate sector, for extended and specialized press release services. They have various types of press release services, which you can find out from their web site.

List of Good Free Press Release Agencies
PRlog.org
PR.com
Pressitt.com (free social media press release)
Exactrelease.com
Live-pr.com
24-7pressrelease.com

E-Mail, Auto Responder Service

Getresponse.com

Getresponse provides a host of services packaged in to one, for an affordable monthly fee. These include, email marketing, spit testing - up to 5 versions of your subjects, design, and content, free online surveys and email analytics. The features include responsive email designer, autoresponders, email creator, landing page creator, social sharing, email analytics (intelligence), list booster, form builder, QR code generator , in all 30 features are included in their package.

MailChimp.com

In case you don't need all the above extra features, you need only email marketing service, then Mailchimp is a better option since their fees are lesser than any other service provider.

Mobile Text Messaging Service

For any business, whether local or global, mobile marketing is a necessary option. There is nothing better than geo-targeting prospects in your area through text messaging services. If you make a local internet search, you will be able to find many such service providers in your area. In case you are not able to get any, here is a list of the most popular Mobile Text Messaging service providers.

Trumpia.com

Trumpia is a multichannel marketing software service. The features include, mobile text messaging, email marketing, social media marketing and voice broadcasting.

Eztexting.com

Ezetexting is one of the leading mobile marketing service providers at affordable cost. The beauty of their service is that you can do it yourself, especially, the Text Messaging Service. The costs are reasonable; they are reliable and trustworthy and carry a TRUSTe logo on their website.

Customer Service

Zopim.com

Zopim is a live chat software provider for online and off line businesses. The Professional version is the best suite of packages and contains all the tools you need to provide an effective live chat service. It is affordable and reliable.

Communication Tools

Facebook Messenger and Whatsapp

The Messenger App is totally free for communicating with anyone and can be used for promotional purposes like the Facebook promoted ads. Whereas WhatsApp is for private communication and the law of permission applies. However, you can collect permission from customers and then use it for instant communication with your customers .

However, in my personal view, the Messenger App scores over WhatsApp as the former is totally free and can be used for marketing purposes using Facebook ads. Both messenger and WhatsApp has an active user base of over 1300 million each as in September 2017. Therefore, please take advantage of this media; If you are not familiar with it, take the help of professional marketing promoters like

Skype.com

Skype is part of the Microsoft family and they offer free as well as premium services. It has the following features - free Skype to Skype calls, Low cost calls, and text messages to mobiles and landlines, video call on Skype and Facebook. Free instant messages to your friends, family and colleagues, video messaging. The premium facility is an excellent one for small, medium, or large businesses. They offer plans star ting at 60 mins. 120 mins, 400 mins, unlimited US, and unlimited world packages.

Ringcentral.com

Ring Central operates in USA, Canada and UK. Their products include office, professional and Fax. Under these categories, you have Business SMS, Toll Free Number, Virtual PBX, Auto Receptionist, Conferencing, and Call forwarding features, all these at a reasonable cost.
The most useful tool for a small business is the Toll Free Number. People's perception is that only Fortune 500 companies are able to provide an 800 Number/Toll Free number. However, small organizations especially, ecommerce retailers can use it as a reputation enhancement and customer interaction tool.

Out Sourcing Difficult Jobs

Elance.com

One of the world's best outsourcing firm for any job related to technical and other jobs like SEO, web design, content writing, CMS, Java Scripts, programming, anything to do with your ecommerce or online business including blogging can be outsourced from Elance's vast array of professional providers, of course, for a fee.

There are several other such service providers, but it is more reliable, cost effective, and professional. This company is now taken over by Freelance.com.

Crowd Sourcing

Another important way to get jobs done fast is through crowd sourcing. It gives you various options and can opt for the best according to your choice. You can get all kinds of services done through crowd sourcing. Some important places to look for crowd sourcing are Odesk.com, Crowdspring.com, Mycrowdburst.com, and DesignCrowd.com For people with financial constraints, Fiverr.com is a good alternative. There you can get everything for just $5.

Chapter 10

SAFETY MEASURES FOR ONLINE BUSINESSES

Back up of your Web Site

Please do not forget to back up your web site in a separate devise preferably in an external hard disk with a storage capacity of 2 or 3 Trillion Bites, which you can buy for less than $120. Though, your web host does it regularly, almost on daily basis or in some cases weekly basis, in your own interest, do it on a regular basis, just in case something unfortunate happens e.g. hacking or defacing by enemies.

SSL Certificate

Server Side Lock (SSL) certificates are must for any online ecommerce sites. There are a large number of providers including shared ones. However, instead of the shared SSL certificate, it will be better if you go for your own SSL certificate.

In case you have many sub-domains, it is better to go in for a wildcard SSL certificate, as it will protect your main domain as well as all other sub- domains. This will cost you on an average about $300/per year. The top rated service providers are VeriSign, Comodo, Geotrust and Thawte. Of these, VeriSign is the costliest.

From outside everything looks fine. However, it is in your own interest to take precautionary safety measures to preempt any unwanted threats from hackers, spyware, malware, phishing and identity thefts. Here is a list of some important precautions you should take:

1. Use only original software and not downloaded free software from unverified sources. Take care to protect your computer from hacking, phishing, and use antivirus, anti- spyware software and firewall. Don't forget to get updates regularly. In addition, use strong passwords preferably a combination of alphabets, numerical and special character combination for your password. In case you are using wireless network, then use encryption to protect yourself.

2. Use SSL certificates from reputed providers, with at least 128 bit SSL certificate with EV (Extended Validation triggers the green address bar in high security browsers) but it will be better if you could afford a 256 bit SSL certificate with the EV (extended validation). However, this may cost a few bucks more but worth it.

3. You can also use the Fraud Score service to protect your Credit Card transaction. It does the following for your safety i.e. Scan and Verify to detect any fraudulent orders, check previous events, categorize risks and delivers a score to indicate the level of risk involved with each order.

4. Spam Protection. While using email marketing, ensure that you use spam guard or protection software, installed on the server itself to get rid of unwanted spam mails reaching your website or main box. Most reputed hosts are providing this feature included in their hosting package. If not, buy and install it on the hosting server. Most shopping carts offer the above features as a package or as an add-on feature, for which separate fees are applicable.

Optional Services for Your Business

Hubspot.com

Hubspot provides a suite of software solutions for inbound marketing. These include Blogging, Social Inbox, SEO, Website pages, Calls-to-Action, Landing pages, Forms, Lead Management, Email, Marketing automation, Analytics, and Salesforce sync.

Hootsuite.com

HootSuite is a social media dashboard that helps organizations use the social web to launch marketing campaigns, identify, and grow audience, and distribute targeted messages across multiple channels. Using HootSuite's unique social media dashboard, teams can collaboratively schedule updates to Twitter, Facebook, Linkedin, Wordpress, and other social networks.

Singlefeed.com

SingleFeed's proprietary technology handles feed import, delivery, makes automated corrections via hundreds of feed rules, validates links, and other data attributes, suggests optimization opportunities, and properly categorizes all products for each of the shopping engines supported. SingleFeed automatically delivers optimized data feeds to the highest quality shopping engines like Buy, Google Shopping, Pricegrabber, and NexTag. Working only with the top shopping engines, it ensures online retailers are getting the most qualified traffic.

A/B or Split Testing and Multivariate Testing

Wingify.com

Every web storeowner needs a tool for testing their web site for identifying flaws, if any. For this purpose, you have to hire the services of an A/B testing or popularly known as Split Testing specialists. Split testing is nothing but you test various features of your web store or a particular page of the web site like the landing page.

For example, you may test the headline, the body of the content page, image, the lead form, or the entire landing page including the submit buttons, to identify which works better. Based on the test results you can adjust your campaigns to increase conversion rates. Sometimes, you will have to do the multivariate testing, i.e. the entire page features are tested to gain insights into what works better and which feature converts more.

Therefore, you have to buy the software for A/B testing or hire the split testing or multivariate testing services. There are many venders out there. However, I found that Wingify.com is the best split testing service provider. Some of their customers include Microsoft, Getresponse etc. The service is a SaaS service and the monthly fees are very reasonable.

Business Blog and Ecommerce Templates

At some point of time, you may like to have some exclusive or premium themes for your business blog or ecommerce site and a landing page. The following are the best template providers in terms of value, features, and ease of use. You may check it out and decide.

Themeforest.net
Premiumwp.com
Templatic.com
Mojo-Themes.com

List of Top Shopping Engines
Shopping.com
Shopzilla.com
Pricegrabber.com
Etsy.com
Halfbuy.com
Google shopping(no more free, however, the ad cost, CPC starts at $0.01/click)
Buy.com
Bestbuy.com
Become.com
Bizrate.com
Yahooshopping.com
Nextags.com
Play.com
Shoplocal.com
BingShopping-Free
Woot.com
TheFind.com-Free

Chapter 11

MONETIZING YOUR WEBSITE

In case you wish to monetize your web site or blog, there are a few good programs like Google Adsense (online advertising) and (Admob) for mobile advertising. In addition, you can supplement your income by promoting others products or service as an Affiliate. The income from these sources may be very little, but if you are lucky and you know how to promote these schemes, then it will be a good idea to earn some extra income. However, there is no substitute for your own product or service, which will give you perennial income.

You will come across innumerable schemes floating on the internet sphere, but only very few players are trustworthy, reliable and pay you promptly. A list of the most trusted program names are given in the Essential Tools and Services chapter.

Monetizing program involves extensive planning and research on your part, like writing timely, relevant and useful content, I mean 100 percent original contents and not copied material, published on your website. If you are not able to write by yourself, you can get it done through ghost writers. However, this will cost you some extra bucks. Therefore, calculate the return on investment, so that you do not waste your money and energy.

If you are from USA, a large number of niches fetches good amount of money as commission through Adsense and Admob. Some of the current hot niches are insurance, credit card, and mortgage loans. There are many people, who wish to start a blog site and earn money through advertising (Adsense or Admob or similar advertising programs) or affiliate marketing or doing both. However, how much you earn is a question mark?

Many gullible people fall into the trap of unscrupulous online marketers, claiming to be gurus or business tycoons. If you really want to earn any amount through the above methods, you must have a web site or blog site with your own domain and hosting, but not with someone's free services.

Do not even think of writing some articles and publishing at free sites like article directories or web 2 properties. These will lead you nowhere and you will not earn any income. Instead, if affordable, start your own web/blog site and promote your own product or services. If you don't have any products or service of your own, then think about promoting other peoples products through affiliate marketing. However, remember that there are several fraudsters floating on the internet. Therefore, be careful and align with reputed, trustworthy companies, who will pay you promptly.

Here is a list of most reputed sites you can approach for promoting, products or services, through affiliate marketing. *Be warned, not to follow or join any MLM (multi level marketing) schemes, including but not limited to AMWAY and other cronies, which are mostly frauds.*

Amazon Associates

The pioneer and world's largest online market place for physical and digital goods, is one of the best income generating program out there. It offer an associates program for sending prospects to their site.   In return, you can earn between 4% to 15% commission for each

product bought. I strongly recommend anyone who wants to earn decent income to opt for Amazon associate ship
.

eBay Partner Networks

eBay is the world's biggest auction site selling new as well as used products on auction basis and on fixed price basis. It does not require any introduction as it is so popular with the masses. They have a program called eBay Partner Networks and offer a commission for sending traffic to their sites.

CommissionJunction.com (CJ)

Commission Junction popularly known as CJ, is the largest affiliate network, especially for physical products. They have thousands of products and services, which you can promote according to your interest.

SiteSell.com

Site Sell or popularly known as SBI, is a Canada based service provider. It offers a very comprehensive online business platform for small businesses at an affordable price. Customers receive the entire system with all the features, including a domain name in your name, hosting, brainstorming, blogging, form building, e-commerce compatibility, an e-zine subscription manager, and a host of other features on annual or monthly fee.

ClickBank.com (CB)

Click Bank is a big place where you can sell information products through a large network of Affiliates. It is very different as they sell your digital (info) products through the network of over 100,000 Affiliates. It offers two types of services, viz. product listing, and the other is their Store Front.

Current Most Popular online items

Books, Clothing and Accessories, Shoes, Video and DVDs are the most popular items online right now. I take this opportunity to thank you for taking the time to read this book and wish you all, great success in your endeavors.

REQUEST

If you liked the information contained in this book and found useful, please write an honest review and rate it. However, there is absolutely no obligation. Also, please spread the word about this book amongst your friends, family members, colleagues, social networks and to any other media that you can.